THE
MANAGER'S
GUIDE

to Workplace Safety

ISBN: 978-0-9667569-2-0

Printed in the United States of America.

10 9 8 7 6 5 4 3

Book Design & Layout: The Book Designers

Book Cover Design: Julie Knudsen

Cover image adapted from iStockphoto.com

BST

a ▷ DEKRA company

THE
MANAGER'S
GUIDE
to Workplace Safety

R. Scott Stricoff and Donald R. Groover

**SAFETY IN
ACTION
PRESS**
An imprint of BST

Acknowledgements

This book, like most, owes its existence to more than just the authors. While our names are on the cover, we could not have done this without the support and assistance of many other people.

We would like to thank the many clients we have had the privilege of working with over our years as consultants. Having had the opportunity to help many different organizations, each with its own history, culture, challenges, and constraints, address a wide variety of safety issues has helped us to develop a broad perspective on safety issues.

In addition, our colleagues at BST have been a valuable source of collaboration. With apologies for anyone we forget, we would like to especially thank (in alphabetical order) Don Martin, Larry Russell, Rick Smith, Jim Spigener, and Tom Ward for reviewing and contributing suggestions to various portions of this book. Tyler Groover and David Stricoff were particularly helpful in reading through the complete first draft and helping us recognize gaps and ways to better organize and clarify the material.

Rebecca Nigel edited the complete manuscript in addition to adapting prior writing to create three of the chapters. Creating a coherent book from the writing of two individuals who have very different writing styles is not an easy or enviable task, and Rebecca did a great job.

Last but certainly not least we would like to thank Brenda Groover and Anita Stricoff for tolerating the lifestyle of consultants, keeping the home front in order over the years while we had fun working with our clients.

TABLE OF CONTENTS

INTRODUCTION

For a combined total of more than 70 years the authors have been working with executives, managers, and supervisors to help them improve safety performance. A recurring theme we have observed is that no manager wants people for whom he or she is responsible to get hurt, but few managers have been prepared through their training and development to play meaningful roles in safety.

As we have advised, coached, and trained executives, managers, and supervisors we have periodically looked for a resource that we could provide to help these leaders understand safety management from the perspective relevant to them. Surprisingly, we have consistently failed to find what we were looking for. Some of the resources we find address the details of safety engineering. Others talk in general terms about the contents of safety programs. But what has been lacking is a book that provides practical guidance on what an individual with management responsibility should *do* to support and drive safety excellence. That is the purpose of this book.

This book is designed for everyone who manages people, from the senior executive to the first-line supervisor. It does not assume these individuals want to or need to become technical safety experts, since in point of fact they do not. It does recognize that these individuals cannot delegate safety entirely to others and expect good results, any more than they could do so with production, quality, or other key organizational objectives. It tells managers how to integrate safety into their management responsibilities in a way that is effective and realistic.

This book addresses safety management, and we make a distinction between management and leadership. In its simplest terms, the distinction is that management is about what we do, while leadership is about how we do it. Both safety management and safety leadership are important, and while there is necessarily some overlap in addressing either, this book concentrates on management. Safety leadership has been addressed by the authors and their colleagues in other books and articles.[1]

This book got its start in several "white papers" that the authors wrote to assist managers who we were coaching in safety improvement. Recognizing that individuals may want to get an "A to Z" sense of safety management or may from time to time run into specific issues on which they want guidance, this book is designed to be effective whether it is read from beginning to end or by "cherry-picking" individual chapters. The individual chapters are designed to be easily digestible and practical rather than theoretical in their guidance.

Anyone who manages people has an interest in helping to assure that injuries do not occur. Understanding and using the guidance in this book can help every manager to be more effective in driving safety excellence.

---

[1] *See for example:* Thomas R. Krause, *Leading with Safety*, (Hoboken: Wiley Interscience), 2005; Colin Duncan (ed.), *The Zero Index: A Path to Sustainable Safety Excellence* (Ojai: Safety in Action Press), 2012.

A PERSPECTIVE ON SAFETY: UNDERLYING PRINCIPLES

Many managers have little occasion to think about the underlying principles of safety. There are safety regulations and safety rules, and it is easy to simply accept them and assume that safety is about following rules. But in the same way that achieving results in production, quality, or customer service is about more than rules, the same is true for safety.

There are a few important principles that every manager should understand when it comes to safety. These principles help the manager understand how injuries occur, why seemingly inexplicable rule violations occur, and what a manager can do about these things. The seven chapters of this section discuss these foundational principles.

CHAPTER ONE

THE MANAGER'S ROLE IN SAFETY

Management is about coping with complexity.
—John Kotter

As a manager you have many responsibilities. You have a functional role that contributes to your organization's success, an administrative role to contribute to the management systems that help drive the organization, a human resources role that involves managing and developing your people, and a planning role that involves helping set future directions for the organization. No doubt these things keep you busy.

Beyond those roles mentioned above, you also have a responsibility for the safety of your employees. Everyone in a management role is responsible for helping to assure that each worker returns home daily without injury and in a broader sense has an injury-free career.

Unfortunately, while individuals have many ways to learn how to manage their functions, the organization's administrative procedures, its planning processes, and the management of people, they tend to have few ways to learn how to manage safety. Formal education for managers rarely addresses the key aspects of safety management, and in most organizations the only safety-related training is focused on front-line employees and their tasks. For the manager who sincerely wants to be effective in assuring a safe workplace, this results in a lot of trial and error, and an unnecessarily large amount of reinventing the wheel.

Understanding how to manage safety involves understanding a number of broad concepts and how to apply them.

To begin there are a number of key foundational principles that should guide thinking on safety. These begin with understanding the concepts of potential and exposure, which help change our orientation from retrospective to prospective. We also must understand the role of behavior in safety: how behavior relates to equipment, conditions, and systems in injury causation, and how to understand and influence the at-risk behaviors we see in the workplace. Next is understanding that not all exposure control mechanisms are equally effective and how to think about them. The similarities and differences between the prevention of individual injuries and prevention of major catastrophic events is another important concept. Finally we must understand the value and limitations of rules as a way to drive safety performance.

With those underlying principles as background a manager can begin thinking about how to establish and enforce expectations regarding safety. This begins with thinking through appropriate roles, responsibilities, and accountabilities for managers and supervisors (including non-operations managers) and for safety professionals. It then progresses to the establishment and implementation of "life-saving rules"—those rules that are most directly related to fatalities and serious injuries, and for which the organization will require rigid compliance. Creating life-saving rules often seems like an easy and obvious step, but the complexities and potential pitfalls are numerous. Finally there is the broad question of using discipline related to safety: when to use discipline and how to use discipline, both of which are complicated questions.

As is true in any area of performance, monitoring activity and results are a key source of information for managers. In safety the focus in most organizations has been very heavily on outcome measures (e.g., injury rates), but managers must learn to establish and use leading indicators as well if they hope to manage safety rather than just react to injuries. Managers also must learn to recognize and react appropriately to the difference between exposures with the potential to cause fatalities and life-altering injuries as compared to those that have lesser potential. Managers also must learn to supplement metrics with other sources of information, such as the results of audits or inspections that can provide insight into the effectiveness of safety management systems.

Another important role of the manager is maintaining alignment within the organization around the safety objective. Through feedback to reinforce what is desired and correct what isn't, managers impact specific individuals and groups, and through safety communications managers impact the organization more broadly. Both safety feedback and safety communication can be powerful tools when done well. However managers sometimes unintentionally undermine their safety message and goals by doing things that trivialize safety, and an effective manager understands how to avoid these unintended consequences. An effective manager also recognizes the value of engaging all employees in safety and understands how to do that through meaningful involvement.

Managers also know that they must learn from experience. In safety that means using available data in ways that provide insight and lead to action, while assuring the response to incidents is designed to uncover important lessons. It also means understanding the cognitive "traps" that can lead to poor decision making in safety.

Everything that happens in an organization is influenced by the culture, and a manager concerned with safety will recognize that he helps establish the culture through everything he does and does not do. Understanding the role of culture within which safety management occurs is necessary to get desired results.

This sounds like a lot to learn, and in some respects it is. But the good news is that many managers have walked this path before and there is much known about how to tackle these issues. This book will discuss all of those issues and in so doing help the reader jump-start his effectiveness as a manager concerned about safety.

CHAPTER TWO

UNDERSTANDING EXPOSURE:
The Paramount Importance of Potential

> *Being in compliance with OSHA and ensuring you have a safe workplace are totally different things.*
> —DAN PETERSEN

Safety excellence is directly related to how effective the organization is at controlling exposure to hazards in the configuration of people, process, and technology. In real terms this means applying resources in time, money, and people to exposures. How to do that is a management problem. The task is made significantly more complex when you understand that not all exposures are equal in terms of their potential for high-severity events.

ANATOMY OF AN INJURY

Exposure simply means that there is a state of vulnerability. When we say someone is exposed to disease, that person is in a position where the disease can be contracted—vulnerable to being impacted by the agents that cause the disease. Similarly when someone is exposed to a workplace hazard, that person is vulnerable to being impacted by that hazard. Some exposures result in more serious incidents; some in less serious ones. And many result in no injury at all. Understanding the distinction among the different types of exposure, specifically the different severity potentials that they represent, has a profound impact on how you manage every aspect of safety.

Consider the following example:

Today I went to the hospital to see Sandy. Sandy's family was there and it was a tough visit. I wished I had answers to their questions about how this could have happened. Sandy's leg is shattered and there is a chance it will have to be amputated. Could anyone really have predicted such a fluke event—that so many things would come together at the same time to lead to this outcome?

Sandy is—rather was—a foreman's dream. Twenty years on the job, he was one of those employees you could always count on, always on time, first in and last out. I could give Sandy the toughest assignments, and he never complained. Sure, Sandy had some injuries and close calls, and you had to be on Sandy about following the rules, but never because of the wrong motivation.

This is the first serious injury we've had on site in 28 months—and the first in this department in over four years. We're known within the company as one of the best in safety, and we have the awards to prove it. How could this have happened?

The accident

Sandy was hurt performing a non-routine job in which he and his coworkers needed to lift a piece of steel deck plate to the second level. This was not a job they did all the time. That morning, Sandy's boss told the crew in the safety briefing how important it was that they get the steel plate lifted into place so they could finish up the work on the compressor below it. The operations department needed the compressor back up and running to get the plant started. He thought they could beat the schedule.

On the crew that morning was a new employee who had little experience rigging this type of load, though he was certified. During the investigation, it was discovered that the sling was bad and shouldn't have been in use. It's possible that a more experienced rigger would have caught it. It's also likely that if the team had rigged the load properly the sling would not have been an issue anyway.

Sandy was hurt when he entered the work area before the crew completed the lift. Several people had to have seen him enter the restricted area, but no one invoked the pause work policy. Every employee at the site has the right to pause work if they believe there is a risk present. While it is true that work pauses hardly, if ever, happen, in this instance one would have thought that someone would have stepped up.

The crew had put up a warning sign and told people in the safety briefing that they were making the lift their first item of the day. Sandy should have seen the sign and known not to enter. Now his boss wishes they would have put up the barricades, but they told everyone during the job safety briefing what was going on. This kind of lift takes less than an hour, so the barricades seemed excessive.

PICKING UP THE PIECES

The story about Sandy is fictional, yet in reading it one can see the many instances where potential for a problem became reality. Consider this partial list of factors that were present:

1. A non-routine rigging job being performed an inexperienced rigger;
2. Production pressure levied to get the compressor online;
3. A foreman who "thought" the crew could beat the schedule;
4. Judgment that installing barricades was not needed;
5. A bad sling and a system that allowed its continued use;
6. A pause work policy that no one felt compelled to invoke; and
7. An employee who had to be repeatedly reminded to follow the rules.

Each of the factors above represents potential as each increased the exposure in the situation. The infrequency of life-altering injuries can make them seem random. But look at these events closely, and you will often see contributing factors that have existed for a long time. What resulted in a life-altering injury today may have produced a minor injury or a near miss last year. For many organizations, the full picture of risk doesn't become apparent until the potential becomes reality. This isn't surprising; the cues to significant injury potential can be subtle. Too often, the signals get lost in the noise of outcomes, metrics, and old paradigms.

DEFINING POTENTIAL

Potential refers to the range of outcomes that can result from any one exposure. Whether any of these outcomes actually occur depends on the configuration of conditions and protective measures that coincide with the exposure. While the potential outcomes for many exposures can range from "nothing bad happens" to fatality, the probability of every potential outcome is not the same. Some exposures have higher probability than others for a life-altering injury, fatality, or catastrophic event.

Learning to distinguish between high- and low-potential situations is a key to allocating resources and oversight effectively. The trouble is that potential is just that: something not yet realized. The task is made harder when you consider the outcomes-driven mindset that many organizations bring to safety. We look at what has happened, not what could happen.

To get started at detecting potential, it is helpful to understand the four chief mistakes that can cause leaders to ignore or overlook significant exposures:

Mistake 1: *Judging an exposure's potential by the severity of the injury*

Many managers, when they are first acquainted with safety, are trained to think in terms of outcomes; e.g., an incident happened or it didn't, an injury was serious or it was "minor." This is helpful in many respects—we have to record what really happened and know what steps to take next. But an outcomes-only focus can also limit our ability to prevent future incidents if we're not careful. For example, consider three possible outcomes of a hammer falling from a height of 20 feet:

- The hammer lands five feet from nearby workers.
- The hammer strikes a worker with a glancing blow, causing a small bruise on the shoulder.
- The hammer strikes a worker at the base of the neck just below her hard hat and fractures her vertebrae.

In many workplaces these outcomes would be recorded as a near miss, a first aid case, and a medical case with lost time, respectively. And in most organizations, that outcome would determine the level of follow up. The problem is that while the outcomes are different in each instance, *the outcome potential is exactly the same*. No matter what the actual outcome, this situation and others like it will always need full investigation. Yet in many organizations the opposite occurs, and the outcome of the incident determines the level of follow-up required. Then when it comes to reporting only the outcome would factor into the safety metrics, and important information about exposures with high potential would likely be lost.

Mistake 2: *Assuming that lagging indicators (outcome metrics) show the total exposure that exists organization wide*

When we miss capturing potential at the individual incident level we naturally gravitate toward aggregating and reporting the data we do have (usually outcome statistics). The problem here is that we mistake what we can see to represent everything we can't. If the medical case rate or severity rate is trending downward, leadership can develop a false level of comfort that the chance of a life-altering event is also declining at an equal pace. However frequency of exposure may be increasing or level while the medical case rate declines.

One of leadership's toughest challenges is understanding how to properly measure safety. While lagging indicators such as medical case rate are attractive (due to their availability, simplicity, and regulatory mandates for use), we also know that these indicators are rife with caveats. For example, medical case rates can be declining even when serious injuries and fatality rates are not. Medical case rate also gives no real indication of the rigor being followed in the process safety arena. And experience shows that if enough pressure is placed on medical case rates, people can become creative in how they "manage" an outcome from recordable to non-recordable.

Managing safety effectively requires understanding the level of exposure that exists, and relying on the common outcome measures to do this is like asking to be misled.

Mistake 3: *Believing that all injuries and exposures have the same potential to be serious or fatal*

A 2011 study on serious injury and fatality (SIF) prevention[1] illustrated the importance of identifying SIF potential in planning safety strategy. The study, which analyzed data from several multinationals, found that the causes and correlates of serious injury and fatality events are usually different than those of less serious injuries. It also found that the potential for serious injury is low for the majority on average (about 80%) of non-SIF injuries.

In other words, *traditional safety efforts often fail to address high-severity potential injuries because they're not designed to.*

Consider two incidents that have produced the same outcome, a broken wrist:

[1] BST, *New Findings on Serious Injuries and Fatalities*, 2011. Available at www.bstsolutions.com.

Incident A	Incident B
An employee stumbles and falls while walking across a paved parking lot. She fractures her wrist in bracing for the impact.	An employee reaches into an auger that moves unexpectedly. It catches the employee's hand and fractures his wrist.

These two incidents have completely different potential, but identical outcomes. If Incident A were to happen 100 more times, it is very unlikely to result in an outcome much worse than a fractured wrist. If Incident B were to happen 100 more times, there is a very good chance there would be loss of limb or life.

Managers who understand safety will recognize that outcome does not indicate potential and will seek to understand which exposures reflect the highest potential. This is addressed further in chapter 17.

Mistake 4: Devoting resources disproportionately to low-potential exposures versus high-potential exposures

Where there are outcome-based measurement systems, incident investigations tend to be triggered by the actual severity of the immediate event rather than by its potential. This approach leads organizations to spend significant time and resources on activities that may or may not impact actual exposure to serious injury. Reporting and investigation of every event is important. At the same time, the manager's role is to carefully weigh the scope and depth of the investigation needed so that resources are applied most effectively.

Consider again the broken wrist example outlined in Mistake 3. In incident A the employee fell while walking at the same level. In most cases a physical inspection of the accident scene and one-on-one discussion with the injured employee to determine if there were any underlying physical causes would represent sufficient investigation. It is even likely that no action items will be required as a result of the incident.

Incident B on the other hand requires an exhaustive investigation that identifies immediate and root causes and that results in significant and meaningful action items. This investigation needs to occur even if the machine cycled unexpectedly but did not result in an injury.

The failure to differentiate events by potential applies to near miss reporting as well. Some systems generate reporting that treats all near misses equally. While reporting of all near misses is highly valuable, even when no injury occurs, it is important to identify those where the potential in a near miss is high and to trigger the appropriate level and scope of investigation and response for those cases.

This "focus on everything equally" mentality can also affect safety processes designed to identify exposure before an incident occurs (e.g., observation systems, audits, and housekeeping inspections). These processes can easily and predictably devolve into only detecting the "easy to find" exposures. Emphasis of prevention then becomes behaviors or conditions that have low-potential outcomes, with an unintentional de-emphasis on high-potential exposures.

MOVING AWAY FROM THE MISTAKES

Managers need to learn to think in terms of exposure and its potential, and to be sure that safety strategies are based on these considerations. A potential focus has implications ranging from the way prevention programs are designed and implemented to the way we measure and assess success. This way of thinking offers some important benefits, including:

1. Making the best use of resources

If your organization is like most, you have a limited amount of resources and they all need to be focused on the most crucial activities. Recognizing differences in potential and allocating resources accordingly allows you to get more value from the time invested.

2. The development of new metrics
A true potential focus naturally drives the development of leading indicators to supplement existing lagging indicators.

3. Greater employee confidence that serious incidents are less likely to occur
Front-line workers, who are closest to the work, often have a deeper and clearer understanding of potential than higher-level leadership. Front-line workers experience the "near misses" and know the "luck" that is involved in escaping serious injury in these cases. They also see when a disproportionate level of effort is expended in researching and investigating low-potential incidents. When front-line workers see real focus placed on the highest potential for injuries, they recognize that there is true commitment to safety improvement.

CHAPTER THREE
WHY PEOPLE GET HURT:
Behavior vs. Equipment/ Conditions

> *You can't feel good about what you're doing if you're not sending people home safely in the process.*
> —PAPER COMPANY EXECUTIVE

Why do people keep getting hurt? It is a question every leader has probably asked sometime in their career, probably more than once and probably in frustration. Are injuries the result of behavior, conditions, culture, or systems? The answer is sometimes yes to all four, sometimes a combination of two or three, and sometimes yes to only one. The only real way to answer the question of why people get hurt is through an investigation.

SAME INJURY, DIFFERENT CAUSES

In any injury there will always be at least one immediate causal factor. The immediate cause may be a behavior, a condition, or both. Below the surface of these immediate causal factors there could be more behavioral and conditional causal factors, cultural factors, and system factors.

Let's look at three examples of employees who injure their wrist while walking into work:

1. An employee arrives at work and while walking to his work location in the designated walkway takes a tumble and strains his wrist. The investigation finds that the area where he was walking

was well lit and the surface was level and free of tripping and slipping hazards. So we can rule out conditions as an immediate casual factor and there is no need to do a root cause analysis.

In the post-incident interview, the worker reports that he was well rested, had a good night's sleep, and was not late or hurrying. The employee was physically fit and had no vision impairment. The employee stated he was looking where he was walking, but that he did have his hands in his pocket. It was a warm morning and not cold out. The employee says that while walking he failed to pick up his feet and took the tumble. Because his hands were in his pockets he was unable to maintain his balance. We can conclude that there is an immediate behavioral causal factor (walking with hands in pockets) that contributed to the incident. Yet any reasonable person would likely not proceed with a root cause investigation on this behavior to try and uncover system and cultural factors. So for this incident there is one cause, a behavior.

2. An employee arrives to work and while walking to her work location in the designated walk way she takes a tumble and strains her wrist. The investigation finds that the area where she was walking was poorly lit. Several of the walkway lights were burnt out and the walking surface was uneven where the asphalt had buckled. We can conclude from this incident that we have two conditional factors that need to be investigated. Both elements will likely lead to the discovery of underlying system and cultural factors.

In the post-incident interview, the worker reports that she was well rested and had a good night's sleep. The employee was physically fit and had no seeing impairment. The employee stated she was looking where she was walking, but that in the area where the incident happened it was particularly dark due to the burnt-out lights. The employee also says that she tripped on a piece of asphalt that was sticking up and took the tumble. She had considered taking another route, but thought walking through the parking lot with people driving into work was more dangerous. We can reasonably conclude that there is not an immediate behavioral factor. It is likely that from the root cause analysis we would find both system (no methodology for inspecting the walkway condition and lighting and/or a breakdown in the system for getting these conditions fixed) and culture (no upward communication about hazardous conditions and normalized risk to mention two) factors.

3. An employee arrives to work and while walking to his work location, he decides to take a shorter route by stepping across a short fence. While stepping across the fence his foot got tangled, and he took a tumble and fell, straining his wrist. The designated walkway was well lit, with all the lights operational, and the asphalt was level and even. From this information we find there are no conditional immediate causes and one immediate behavioral cause (taking a short cut).

   In the interview, the employee states that he was running a bit late, so he had decided to take a shorter, more direct route to the work area. The employee says that he didn't want to be late because the foreman had a contest going regarding everyone being to work on time, and he had been given a written warning about being late once before. The employee says that if he were late then everyone in the crew would lose a pizza lunch. From this interview we can determine that there are root causes to the employee's behavior that include both personal factors and system factors.

While these three events had the same outcome and are simplistic in nature, they do illustrate that when we look at just the outcome, an employee falls walking into work and injures his wrist, there are different immediate and root causal factors. It is easy to jump to conclusions about causation based on the outcome and the superficial characteristics of an event, but to really understand causation we must consider the possible contributions of behavior, systems, conditions, *and* equipment.

CHAPTER FOUR

WHY PEOPLE DO WHAT THEY DO:
Addressing the Behavioral Side of Safety

> *Everything people do makes sense—*
> *we just have to be smart enough to*
> *understand how it makes sense.*
> —MANAGER AT A CHEMICALS PLANT

Most of us are all too familiar with the gap between what we know we should do and what we actually do. We know we would like to be more fit, devote more time to our families, be more patient, and get our important errands done. Nevertheless we often fall short of doing what we intend.

The same is true in the workplace. The way we intend things to be done often differs from how they actually get done. This gap is so much a fact of organizational life that most of us have adapted to it and accept it as inevitable. The good news is, we don't need to—if we understand the principles of behavior, we can solve some of safety's most perplexing problems.

THE MYSTERY OF HUMAN ACTION

In the course of our work, we often hear managers say things such as:

- We have a rule but people don't follow it.
- Anyone could have seen that was a dangerous thing to do.

- We've trained people again and again, but they still don't
  do it correctly.

If any of these frustrations sound familiar, you are in good company. Many managers see that the immediate demands or consequences (good and bad) of the workplace are a stronger influence on employees than rules or policies, even when breaking those rules poses risk of injury. The good news is that human behavior is not random or arbitrary. It is shaped by predisposing factors and by results—the *antecedents* and *consequences*. Systems influences, perceptions of risk, the norms of culture, organizational consequences, and the example of leaders are among the factors that influence decisions about safety-related behavior. When these organizational elements are poorly aligned with standards, deviation from safe practice is not far behind. Yet, in cases where the intention is to prevent exposure to accidents and injury, closing this gap is an imperative and it starts with understanding what the various pieces are.

A manager who understands and knows how to use these concepts can have huge impact on safety (as well as in other areas.)

WHAT DRIVES BEHAVIOR

In behavioral science terms, a behavior is any observable act. It is not inherently good or bad. Putting on a seat belt, wearing fall protection when working at elevation, telling a subordinate that he or she did a good job (or correcting them), and removing a guard from a machine are all examples of behavior.

Many of the things we have traditionally done in safety have been intended to influence behavior. We train people, write procedures, post warnings, and do safety briefings in an effort to assure that people act safely—in other words, to influence their behavior. The frustrations noted at the start of this chapter (and many others like those) arise from the fact that these attempts to influence behavior are often not as effective as we would like. And that is because they are usually implemented without consideration of what really influences behavior.

Antecedents and consequences influence behavior:

- Antecedents are the events and circumstances that precede and predispose a behavior, for example, rules, training, the availability or condition of equipment, and employee knowledge or culture.
- Consequences are results that follow a behavior, including any event or change, for example, saving time, approval from peers or boss, convenience, the job gets done without incident, and even injury.

Both antecedents and consequences, and how they are perceived, lead to a behavior. While many organizations focus their attention on antecedents (through training, signs, slogans, and admonitions), it is really the consequences to the individual that drive behavior. Antecedents predispose a behavior and drive behavior to the extent that they predict consequences of the behavior.

To illustrate what we mean, consider the following example:

At the end of his shift, an employee enters a work area to perform one last task before going home. The job requires the use of eye protection, a fact that is prominently noted on signs posted at the entrance. Still, the employee walks past the signs and goes to perform his task. It's only a few minutes, the employee thinks, and it would take more time to go get the safety glasses than it would to just do the job. In addition, the employee reasons, the exposure must surely be minimal. Waving to the area supervisor, who greets the employee with a friendly nod before returning to his own task, the employee finishes his work and goes home for the day without incident.

When it comes to any personal protective equipment (PPE), we generally establish rules and procedures for its use, train people in those rules and procedures, and enforce those rules by noting when individuals fail to follow the rule and taking some corrective action. As most managers have seen at one time or another, this approach generally results in imperfect compliance with the rule.

Like all behaviors, the behavior of not wearing PPE (the behavior we wish to eliminate) is influenced by antecedents and consequences. Analyzing the behavior in this example (Table 4-1) it is clear that the most powerful consequence controlling the PPE behavior is the immediate, positive reinforcement of getting the job done in a short amount of time. The worker is looking forward to the end of the day and completing the job and has a friendly, if brief, exchange with the supervisor. These positive social consequences far outweigh the very weak negative consequences—getting caught, being reprimanded, or suffering eye injury. These negative consequences are weak because they are rare outcomes relative to the number of times someone can fail to use eye protection without suffering any negative consequences.

Table 4-1. *Analysis of a behavior.*

Antecedents	Behavior	Consequences
Availability and condition of safety glasses	Not wearing eye protection	Save time
Peers don't use eye protection		Comfort
Does not believe he will get caught		Convenience
In a hurry		Peer approval
End of shift, looking forward to going home		Gets caught/ reprimanded
Has seen supervisors look the other way with regard to PPE use		Suffers eye injury
Doesn't believe that one time failure will result in injury		

RANKING CONSEQUENCES

The power of consequence is based on three things: timing, certainty, and outcome. A consequence that occurs immediately upon performance of the behavior is more influential than one that occurs later. A consequence that is certain to occur is more influential than one that is uncertain. A consequence that is positive to the individual will encourage repetition of that behavior, while a consequence that is negative to the individual will discourage that specific behavior (but not encourage any specific replacement).

Going back to our PPE example, the first consequence (injury) would probably occur immediately if it occurred, but is uncertain, and is negative. The second (discipline) might occur immediately or later, but again is uncertain and negative. These consequences are both uncertain—we can fail to use PPE many times without being injured, and unless a supervisor sees us working without the PPE and takes action we will not be disciplined. However each of the other three consequences occurs immediately, is certain and is positive. Since soon, certain, and positive consequences are the most powerful in driving a behavior, it should not be surprising that achieving 100% compliance with PPE use is difficult.

Understanding that behavior is based on logical and identifiable influences puts us in position to reduce undesired behavior and to encourage desired behavior. We can work to reduce antecedents that encourage undesired behavior and increase antecedents that encourage desired behavior. We can also work to eliminate or minimize consequences driving undesired behavior and add consequences supporting desired behavior. In the PPE example, we can try to find more comfortable PPE and make sure that it is always available when needed. We can provide recognition for its use. We can enlist front -line workers in peer-based programs to encourage its use.

PUTTING KNOWLEDGE
OF BEHAVIOR TO WORK

With an understanding of the concepts, how does a manager put this into practical use? There are four steps to applying behavioral thinking to the reduction of at-risk behavior in the workplace:

- UNDERSTAND—The first step in reducing at-risk behavior is to understand the behavior you want to address and the antecedents and consequences that are influencing the at-risk behavior.

- VERIFY—The second step is to verify that your understanding of antecedents and consequences is correct. A group of managers and supervisors and safety professionals may believe they understand the antecedents and consequences, but it is important to be sure you have identified these from the perspective of the people performing the at-risk behavior. This may be done by talking to a cross section of front-line workers, but if a behavior-based safety process exists there will be data to support this activity found in the comments associated with observations of at-risk behavior.

- ADJUST—The third step is to identify and implement changes to the antecedents and consequences that are influencing the behavior of interest.

- ASSESS—The fourth step is to assess the impact of the changes and repeat the process if the desired result is not being achieved.

APPLYING BEHAVIOR ANALYSIS ELSEWHERE

This understanding and approach can be put into use to help address a number of different challenges managers face in safety improvement efforts. Several of these are discussed below:

Compliance

The most obvious application is in improving compliance with safety rules. Where non-compliance is a problem, analysis of the behavior of not following the rule often provides important insight into why. While it is often easy for managers to assume that non-compliance results from employees simply wanting to be defiant or uncooperative, analysis of non-compliance behavior usually shows that there are logical reasons for non-compliance, and when those are understood the issues can be addressed.

Incident investigation

Most incidents involve a behavioral component, and it is common for that to be identified in an investigation, and then addressed in recommendations for increased or repeat training of employees. A manager who understands behavior will recognize the importance of ensuring that an incident investigation uncovers the antecedents and consequences that drove contributing behavior, and developing recommended actions that address those antecedents and consequences. Only through this type of analysis will the real basis of at-risk behavior be understood and eliminated.

Pre-planning

When planning for an atypical task or developing job procedures, understanding of the antecedents and consequences influencing workers who will be doing the task allows for creation of a plan that encourages desired behavior. Anticipating the antecedents and consequences that could drive undesired behavior in performing the task allows one to avoid those and instead create reinforcement for the desired task behaviors.

Training

Managers often express frustration because they invest significant resources in training but the trainees do not seem to absorb what was intended. A more insightful view is to recognize that people do what they do on the job because of the antecedents and consequences in place. Training may help to address some of those antecedents (e.g., lack of knowledge of how to do the desired behavior), but training alone will not address the consequences that are driving behavior in most situations. When training is done as part of a structure in which the desired behaviors are taught and then are reinforced through what occurs in the workplace, behavior change is more likely to occur.

Coaching

When a manager takes a coaching approach to helping a subordinate improve performance, understanding of behavior helps make the coaching interaction more effective. The manager who understands the role of antecedents and consequences can help the subordinate understand what is influencing his or her behavior, and together they can identify ways to create consequences that will reinforce the desired behavior.

THE POWER OF BEHAVIOR

Understanding that behavior is driven by logical and identifiable influences opens up new ways for a manager to address safety improvement. Rather than believing at-risk behavior to be inevitable or untouchable, the manager who uses behavior analysis can see why things happen as they do and implement specific plans for improvement.

CHAPTER FIVE
EXPOSURE CONTROL DECISIONS:
The Hierarchy of Controls

Action expresses priorities.
—MAHATMA GANDHI

Fundamentally, improving safety is about removing exposures. Managers have the authority and the resources to execute safety improvements on a much larger scale than individual workers. In some cases, exposures require your involvement in order to be remedied at all, for example when hazards are created by the design of machinery or work processes. As your team identifies and assesses exposures —through incident investigation, hazard analysis, workplace inspections, audits, observations, or by analyzing the design and installation of new equipment or processes, or a variety of other things—your job as a manager is to determine the most appropriate response to those exposures. The good news is that there is a framework that provides a helpful guide to thinking about and executing exposure reduction in a variety of situations: the hierarchy of controls.

THE HIERARCHY OF CONTROLS
The goal of exposure reduction is to isolate the worker, as much as possible, from exposure to risk. Some ways of doing this are more effective and reliable than others. The logic essential for determining which controls are necessary is called the hierarchy of controls. While the logic is simple—use the highest level of control whenever possible, and supplement with lower levels of control as required—the application of the hierarchy of controls

must be carried out with consideration given to actual budgets
and financial realities along with the urgency for the solution.
Sometimes, multiple controls are required. Lower level controls,
at times, have to be used as stopgaps until higher level controls
come on line.

The principle of behavioral reliability

The easiest and least expensive way of reducing exposure often
appears to be requiring use of personal protective equipment
(PPE), for example hard hats, face shields, or respiratory protective
equipment. But is this always the best way? Organizations often
jump to the use of PPE without fully considering the limitations of
this approach.

Of all of the approaches available for reducing exposure in the
workplace, PPE is one of those that has the highest degree of *behavioral variability* influencing its effectiveness. That is, the effectiveness
of PPE is heavily dependent on it being used correctly every time
and maintained correctly at all times. This makes its effectiveness
highly dependent on each user and those responsible for providing
and maintaining it exhibiting the right behaviors to assure protection
each and every time it is used. While that is not impossible, it makes
use of PPE more subject to failure than (for example) redesigning the
work to eliminate the exposure.

Eliminating a hazard is at the opposite extreme of behavioral
reliability. Once a hazard is removed, the worker is not exposed to
that hazard regardless of anyone's behavior. For example, if a hazardous chemical is added to a process by manually pouring and we install
hard piping to transfer the chemical instead, we have eliminated the
exposure to spills or splashes. Similarly, if you install a permanent
work platform with guard rails so that a ladder need not be used to
reach a sampling port, the exposure associated with potentially falling from the ladder is eliminated.

LEVELS OF PROTECTION

It is probably apparent from these examples that in most cases opting to require PPE is a faster and less expensive (at least in the short term) approach, and that is why it is often used despite its having lower behavioral reliability. However that does not make it the best choice.

The choices available as an exposure reduction strategy are broader than simply use PPE or elimination. And different types of control strategy offer different levels of behavioral reliability. The categories of exposure reduction strategy form a Hierarchy of Controls as follows:

PPE

There is a variety of types of PPE such as hard hats, protective gloves and suits, respiratory protective equipment, fall protection equipment, face shields, and flame-retardant clothing. PPE is widely used in a variety of applications and has a useful place as part of the overall safety strategy. It also has the lowest behavioral reliability.

Administrative controls

Administrative controls entail the use of procedures to reduce exposure. Depending on the nature of the exposure, procedures may entail such things as requiring work permits for high-hazard tasks or limiting the amount of time an individual may be exposed to a hazard. While more reliable than PPE, this approach is still highly dependent on behavior as the procedure will do little good unless it is followed rigorously and consistently. For managers, this means you must provide consistent oversight to ensure absolute compliance.

Engineering controls

Engineering controls entail the use of hardware systems to reduce exposure, for example enclosures to isolate equipment, ventilation systems, machine guards, and safety interlocks. While there is still some behavioral variation in the effectiveness of this approach (since the controls must be kept in place and maintained), the reliability is higher than with PPE or Administrative Controls.

Substitution/Elimination

As described above, elimination of a hazard removes exposure to that hazard and is not subject to behavioral variability. Of course the replacement may introduce different exposures that then require appropriate mitigation measures.

APPLYING THE HIERARCHY OF CONTROLS

Your objective as a manager is to control every exposure with the most behaviorally reliable approach possible, where both technical and economic feasibility often enter into the decision about what is possible. Make it a habit to question decisions made about exposure control strategies. Were higher reliability alternatives considered? If relatively low reliability solutions were selected, are there longer-term alternatives that will employ higher reliability strategies? While not every exposure can be addressed through elimination, neither should every exposure be addressed through PPE.

By understanding the hierarchy of controls and what it says about the reliability of exposure control approaches, a manager can help to drive continuous improvement in his or her organization.

CHAPTER SIX

CATASTROPHIC EVENT PREVENTION:
Taking a Comprehensive Approach

When people lose an appreciation of how their safety systems were intended to work, safety systems and controls can deteriorate, lessons can be forgotten, and hazards and deviations from safe operating procedures can be accepted …People can forget to be afraid.

——BP Texas City Safety Review Panel

A catastrophic event involves a major failure that results in multiple losses of life and/or substantial damage to property or the environment. Major events in recent years have highlighted the contrast and connection of personal safety (preventing employee injuries and fatalities on the job) and process safety (preventing fires, explosions, uncontrolled releases of hazardous materials). Of most concern to managers is the fact that organizations can perform well in personal safety while significant vulnerabilities in process safety persist.

Prevention of these events requires an understanding of the interaction between technical and organizational factors, and a willingness to address organizational issues in addition to technical issues.

KEY ELEMENTS OF PROCESS SAFETY
Prevention of catastrophic events from the unexpected release of materials or energy is called process safety in the chemical and

petroleum industries, but is a concern in many other industries as well. Its study and application has received significant attention in the last 25 years, with major incidents (e.g., Piper Alpha and Bhopal) giving rise to new rules and practices. But despite this attention, major catastrophic incidents in the chemical process industries (e.g., Texas City, Deepwater Horizon) and in other industries (e.g., Upper Big Branch mine, San Bruno gas pipeline explosion, Chatsworth rail accident) have continued to occur. Retrospective views on these events have consistently shown organizational cultures that resulted in systems breakdown.

This pattern pointedly tells us that catastrophic event prevention must make the same migration as that of personal safety in recent years—one of recognition that systems are only as effective as the culture in which they operate. We know that culture shapes behavior. And behavior is how systems are implemented.

Numerous widely recognized technical and management systems have been designed to help prevent catastrophic events. These systems were articulated and codified in a series of activities sponsored by groups such as the AIChE's Center for Chemical Process Safety, the ACC's Responsible Care program, the American Petroleum Institute, and through individual company efforts. Ultimately, OSHA incorporated these systems into a standard on process safety management in the U.S. The key technical and management systems for preventing catastrophic events, which are applicable to all industries with catastrophic event potential, are:

- PROCESS SAFETY INFORMATION—Maintaining accurate and complete information on materials, equipment, processes, etc.

- PROCESS HAZARD ASSESSMENT (PHA)— Evaluating systematically the hazards associated with operational systems using one of a number of techniques that help assure thorough review.

- OPERATING PROCEDURES—Having and maintaining procedures to govern operations.

- TRAINING—Assuring that individuals working in potentially hazardous operations are trained regarding the hazards and their control.

- CONTRACTOR MANAGEMENT—Using safety as a criterion in selection of contractors and assuring that contractors understand the hazards of the owner's operation and have appropriate procedures to control hazards in their own work.

- MECHANICAL INTEGRITY—Assuring that critical equipment is maintained in good condition.

- NON-ROUTINE WORK AUTHORIZATIONS—Having procedures to assess the hazards of and to control work in other than normal operations (e.g., start-up, shut down).

- MANAGEMENT OF CHANGE (MOC)—Assuring that all changes to equipment, materials, and processes are assessed for possible safety impact and result in updates to procedures and process safety information as needed.

- INCIDENT INVESTIGATION—Determining the root causes of incidents with appropriate follow up action based on findings.

- EMERGENCY PLANNING AND RESPONSE— Preparation for response to emergency situations.

- SELF-AUDITS—Periodically assuring that these systems and procedures are in place, in use, and up to date.

CREATING THE RIGHT CONTEXT FOR SAFETY SYSTEMS

Virtually all catastrophic events in man-made systems are related to technical failures made possible by organizational failures. This explains why catastrophic events continue to occur despite widespread implementation of sophisticated technical and management systems. Investigations of the Deepwater Horizon and Texas City events in the petrochemical process industries have pointed to issues with *organizational safety*—the context within which technical and management systems function. It is important to recognize that this issue transcends the industries traditionally thought to need process safety management. Incidents such as the Chatsworth train accident, Upper Big Branch, and San Bruno share the same issues as Deepwater Horizon and Texas City—the failure of organizations to keep pace with technology in the management of safety.

Managers need to recognize organizational safety as a whole, understand how it must be managed, and identify where it tends to break down. In thinking about organizational safety, managers need to consider seven primary questions:

1. Do people throughout the organization understand the difference between personal safety and prevention of catastrophic events? If not, they may mistake good performance in personal safety with good control of the potential for catastrophic events.
2. Do we have the right technical and management systems in place and do they get implemented as intended (and how are they monitored)? Ultimately what happens day-to-day is more important than the design intent of these systems.
3. Does our culture support consistent and rigorous use of safety technical and management systems? Culture determines the way things are really done in the organization, and if the culture does not support key systems, the systems are bound to break down.
4. Do our leaders act in ways that promote identification of exposure and reduction of risk? There are key leadership behaviors that can help assure effective hazard recognition, evaluation, and control. If leaders are not aware of these and actively practicing them, technical and management systems are likely to be compromised.
5. Do our "consequence management" systems support the activities critical to prevention of catastrophic events? The

way performance is assessed, promotions awarded, and recognition and rewards distributed are all examples of how key systems influence perceptions of what is truly important to succeed in an organization.

6. Do we have the right skills available for supporting all aspects of safety? Do we assign roles and responsibilities in a way that assures clarity, alignment, coordination, and communication? Prevention of catastrophic events is generally a multifunctional effort. This requires careful consideration of how the various participants interact and collaborate.

7. Are the metrics in place to detect changes in exposure and assure focus on key processes and procedures? If the only metrics in use for safety are those addressing personal safety, the organization will be unable to detect trends in catastrophic event potential.

COMPREHENSIVE PROCESS INCIDENT PREVENTION

Organizations must move beyond the traditional technical and management systems, building upon those systems in implementing a comprehensive approach to the prevention of catastrophic events. This approach has four components: Anticipation, Inquiry, Execution, and Resilience.

Anticipation

Anticipation refers to having an organization with the systems and culture to be sensitive to the recognition of "weak signals" that may be indicative of increased risk of catastrophic events.

An organization that is strong in Anticipation will have mechanisms to capture information from a variety of sources. Once captured, the various types of information that can be early indicators must be accessible and structured in a way that allows analysis of patterns across various types of data. Even when systems are in place, it is incumbent upon the organization to assure that the systems function as intended. It is important for leaders to encourage individuals to be alert for weak signals and to reinforce this behavior. Finally the information gathered must be used effectively. This requires having people with appropriate skills who are given appropriate encouragement and attention.

Inquiry

Inquiry involves making effective use of information to analyze, understand, and plan mitigation of risks. Traditional process safety management includes a number of elements (such as process-hazard analysis, pre-startup safety review, management of change) designed to evaluate and plan for control of hazards and risks. However there are common (but often undetected) cultural characteristics that can undermine the effectiveness of these efforts and leave the organization vulnerable.

Cognitive bias refers to the tendency we all have to rely on intuitive rather than analytical thinking in order to process information efficiently.[1] Where cognitive bias becomes particularly problematic for catastrophic event prevention is that our methods for systematic hazard analysis can be influenced and can cause us to underestimate or even miss entirely potential failure scenarios. In addition, the routine operational decision-making that occurs day-to-day can be influenced by cognitive bias, leading to unintended increases in risk.

While awareness of cognitive bias helps to counteract its effect, the best way to guard against the insidious effects of cognitive bias is to have an organizational culture that combats it. There are also specific skills involved in asking the right question in the right way to get the right data.

---

[1] Cognitive bias is discussed further in chapter 28.

Execution

Excellent hazard identification and assessment, as well as hazard control efforts, can be undermined if the programs and practices are not followed as intended. While many organizations use periodic audits to provide a check on implementation, the key to assuring consistent and ongoing activity is managers who systematically monitor, reinforce, and verify effective program execution.

Resilience

Upset conditions occur from time to time in any system. Resilience refers to the organization's ability to react in ways that prevent upset conditions from becoming catastrophic events, and then learning from the experience. This has a major influence on ultimate results.

One requirement for strong resilience is knowledge; that is, do people at various levels have a broad enough understanding of the operation so that they can make good judgments in case of emergency. Some organizations approach this through use of extensive sets of rules and procedures. The second requirement for resilience is willingness, and this relates directly to culture. Simply put, people are less likely to take action on their own initiative if they are not confident that the organization will support them.

PREVENTING CATASTROPHE

The discussion above emphasizes the importance of supplementing systems with specific leadership behaviors to create and sustain the culture that leads to prevention of catastrophic events. Focused initiative is often needed to introduce these leadership behaviors in a way that will integrate them effectively with other safety efforts and assure their use in day-to-day activities.

CHAPTER SEVEN

REGULATION AND RULES:
Necessary But Not Sufficient

Rules are not necessarily sacred, principles are.
—FRANKLIN D. ROOSEVELT

In some organizations there is a feeling that regulatory compliance means safety is well managed. In other organizations there is a view that the path to zero injuries is through creating and enforcing more and more rules. In reality neither of these ideas is valid. When it comes to managing safety, it is essential to understand the role of regulations and where they fit in the big picture.

REGULATIONS–THE LEAST COMMON DENOMINATOR

Government regulations in workplace safety have played an important role in establishing a minimum acceptable standard for places of employment. They create a "baseline" that all employers are required to meet, and historically that has raised the bar for a segment of the workplaces.

There are two types of regulations: specifications and performance standards. Both types are mandatory. The distinction is in telling you how to do it or not:

- SPECIFICATIONS dictate what should be done. For example, the requirement that a guard rail around a floor opening must be 42-inches high and the requirement that a fire extinguisher must be inspected monthly are specifications.

- PERFORMANCE STANDARDS, on the other hand, are more programmatic in nature and indicate what must be done without specifying how. For example, the requirement that hazard analysis be done on a process using hazardous chemicals is a performance standard, as it leaves open issues such as what technique should be used for analysis.

Government regulations must apply broadly, and due to a combination of technical, economic, and political considerations specification-type regulations tend to be aimed at the most egregious issues. Regulations do not drive safety excellence; rather, they tend to reduce the worst safety deficiencies. Compliance with these regulations does not imply that exposures are well controlled or that systems to assure exposures remain controlled are in place.

Compliance with performance standards in many ways provides even less assurance of safety excellence. Because performance standards intentionally allow for interpretation of how to best comply, they are very difficult to enforce consistently.

The bottom line is that compliance with government regulations is an expectation of all organizations but should not be confused with endorsement that a strong and effective safety program is in place.

TAKING THE EASY WAY OUT

Often we see a plethora of rules and procedures within an organization. Basic expectations and methods are spelled out in rules. Then an incident occurs and in response a new rule or procedure is adopted. Then individual departments feel the need to create their own customized versions of rules and procedures. Then a new corporate initiative will be launched and rules and procedures written to implement it. Before long the organization has a huge number of rules and procedures—far more than anyone can be expected to really remember. Now incident investigations find that all applicable rules or procedures were not followed, and unfortunately all too often the reaction is to create additional rules, see-ing the employee as the problem and not really looking for root causes. As the number of rules grows, so does the likelihood of inconsistency among them, resulting in greater apparent non-compliance with the rules. This destructive cycle leads to frustration on the part of both man-agement and front-line workers, and makes effective safety improve-ment difficult.

Of course it is important to have procedures and rules to spell out expected practices and provide a basis for training. However the error that managers make is to think that writing a rule or procedure actu-ally changes what happens in the field. Writing rules is not a panacea.

PUTTING RULES TO WORK FOR YOUR ORGANIZATION

There are a number of factors to assess when considering the role of rules and procedures in advancing safety.

Volume

A good place to start is by examining the sheer volume of rules that exist in the organization. If the volume is so large that it is not real-istic to expect people to really know what all of the rules say, then you can assume that people will act in a way consistent with what they think the rules intend, and you cannot assume that the rules are really driving behavior. In this situation, what typically happens is that there is a subset of rules that are the ones people really follow, and another (larger) group that are widely considered to be more like guidelines than rules. In this situation, you are better off being clear about which rules are important than you are in letting each individual draw his or her own conclusions.

Consistency

Another consideration is whether rules are consistent among departments and groups. It is not unusual to find situations where people from one department are working immediately adjacent to people from a different department, and because the departments have different rules one person may be (for example) wearing personal protective equipment while the other is not. This type of inconsistency undermines confidence that the rules are really meaningful, and also makes enforcement of the rules very difficult.

How we train people

If new workers are trained in the rules and are assumed to know them from that point forward, it is unlikely that the rules will be effective. New employees won't immediately retain everything as they are receiving information out of context (i.e., they have not yet experienced the actual job). When they leave training and go on the job they are likely to be exposed to "old hands" who will tell them "the way we really do it." This is especially true when there is not periodic retraining on the rules, which helps to assure that new and experienced employees are hearing the same thing about expectations.

Enforcement

Enforcement of rules helps determine how they are perceived. If a rule is never enforced, it will obviously be seen as optional. If it is enforced inconsistently there will be confusion about the organization's intent, and focus is likely to shift toward trying to understand how to avoid getting caught rather than focusing on how to reduce exposure. If rules are enforced only following an injury the entire rules structure will be perceived as simply a mechanism for pushing blame to employees. Proper enforcement of rules is critical, and is discussed at length in the chapters on discipline (chapters 13 and 14.)

Why rules aren't followed

Most importantly, when rules are not followed do we understand why? As discussed in chapter 4 in most cases when behavior is inconsistent with what is desired by management there are good reasons that can be discovered and addressed. Simply attributing non-compliance to willfully poor employees and assuming that means injuries are inevitable is a naïve approach.

PUTTING RULES IN CONTEXT

Regulations and rules are important as a piece of the overall safety effort, but an effective manager understands their limitations and does not assume that simply writing and disseminating rules will handle all you need to do in safety. The manager's role is to understand the role rules and regulations play in their organization, assure alignment of existing rules with the organization's safety objectives, and help others put them in the right context.

ESTABLISHING AND ENFORCING EXPECTATIONS

One of the roles of managers is to organize the work, assuring that appropriate staffing is in place, all responsibilities are assigned, and that people are accountable for performance. Assuring these things for safety is no less important than it is for other performance areas.

However we often see confusion about these things in safety. In a surprising number of organizations, there is ambiguity about the division of roles and responsibilities and duties among line and staff personnel, what types of safety goals should be established for individual managers and supervisors, and how to balance the desire for employee engagement and collaboration with the idea of discipline and accountability.

To be effective in safety, managers and supervisors must have a clear understanding of these issues, and the six chapters of this section provide guidance on how to address the issues.

CHAPTER EIGHT

RESPONSIBILITY AND ACCOUNTABILITY

Safety isn't a priority. It's a precondition.
—PAUL O'NEILL

Who is responsible for employee safety?

Managers and supervisors are responsible for assuring that every employee has a successful shift and safely completes their workday. Managers and supervisors control the work environment and work rules, and drive the culture that influences how the work gets done.

Too often we hear managers say the solution for improved safety performance is for the workers to step up and watch out for themselves, follow the rules, and tell their peers when they are doing something wrong. When managers single out the employee's need to change and step up as the answer it is an abdication of leadership responsibility. It would be unacceptable to say the answer to underperforming production is that the workers need to step up and take responsibility.

WHO OWNS SAFETY?

Managers and supervisors need to recognize that safety is an integral part of their job in the same way as are production, quality, and expense control. Management is responsible for safety just as they are for production and all performance areas. It is what people sign up for when they agree to accept a management role.

What about individual front-line workers?

Do the workers have a role in our success, safety, and otherwise? Clearly the answer is yes. But as management we have a responsibility to create a physical work environment and culture where the employees are able to work safely and are motivated to work safely.

What is the role we desire for the hourly employees in safety? First we want employees to follow our rules and procedures. Ideally they would also be willing to pause a job if they were concerned about the level of exposure. This is a narrow focus on safety of self. In a higher functioning culture we would see employees approaching their peers about safety concerns. Finally, in the highest functioning culture we would see employees approaching not only their peers but anyone about safety concerns.

But to a large extent it is management that determines whether employees will play these roles.

We want employees to follow rules, but do we seek to assure that the rules can be followed? That rewards and recognition do not flow to those who take shortcuts? That managers and supervisors set the right example by following the rules themselves? That visitors are informed of and expected to follow the rules? That feedback (and, ultimately, other consequences) is given consistently to those who do and do not follow rules?

We want employees to be willing to pause a job if they are concerned about the level of exposure. If an employee does this what is the reaction of management? Is the employee made to feel uncomfortable in defending his or her decision or thanked for taking action?

We want employees to watch out for each other and approach one another if they see a safety concern. Do we communicate to workers about the importance of this and how it is valued by the organization? Do we train workers on how to recognize increased exposure?

We want employees to take that even further and approach anyone—executive, manager, contractor, visitor—when they see that person at-risk. But how do managers interact with front-line workers? Do they engage workers and invite comments and discussion? Are they defensive when workers express concerns?

While we want and need participation from front-line workers in safety, a necessary first step is for management to model the desired behavior. It isn't appropriate to demand high function behaviors from the workforce when management doesn't lead the way.

What about the safety department?

If attendance is poor do we blame the HR manager? If expenses are high do we blame the CFO? Similarly, if safety performance is poor it makes little sense to single out the safety manager for blame.

Safety is ultimately a line management responsibility, and so it is unrealistic to expect anyone in a staff role, such as the safety professional or the HR professional, to manage safety. Line managers should expect to be supported by the safety professional.

But the safety professional should also expect to be supported by line management. The safety professional should be an advocate for safety and a source of both new ideas and of observations that may run counter to the conventional wisdom of the location. The safety professional may have to surface issues that make people uncomfortable. This cannot happen unless the safety professional is sponsored at the highest level of the organization and everyone is clear about both the safety professional's role and their own roles in safety.

The role of the safety professional is discussed in more detail in chapter 9.

CREATING ACCOUNTABILITY

In some organizations "holding people accountable" is understood to mean using discipline or other types of punishment (e.g., smaller or no bonuses or raises) when responsibilities are not fulfilled. This is a narrow and generally ineffective approach, as it focuses on response to failure rather than helping assure success. In effective organizations accountability means ongoing evaluation of performance relative to an established objective, target, or standard and providing feedback and other consequences based on that performance. While we often hear people say that "everyone is responsible for safety," in organizations that excel everyone is accountable for safety.

Set clear goals and expectations

ANTECEDENT

The first step in establishing safety accountability is having clear safety goals and expectations for everyone, at all levels of the organization. Every manager, supervisor, and executive needs to have clear and specific safety goals. (We discuss goal setting in more detail in chapter 10.) For front-line employees, the expectation should be that safety rules will be followed and there will be participation in established safety programs (e.g., taking part in pre-job briefings.)

Note that the focus of accountability is on the safety systems and activities that drive safety outcomes. Historically, many organizations have placed the exclusive focus of accountability on outcomes—that is, they hold managers accountable for the injury rate. This sole focus on outcomes can lead to dysfunctional behaviors since there are many ways to reduce the outcome measure without actually impacting safety—for example, subtly or overtly discouraging reporting, "liberal interpretation" of whether an injury is not work related, or discouraging medical treatment. When individuals' exclusive accountability for safety is the outcome measure the likelihood of seeing these dysfunctional behaviors increases.

Evaluate performance

BEHAVIOR

The second step in accountability is to establish ongoing and objective evaluation of performance relative to an individual's established goals and expectations. The focus of evaluation is on achieving a shared view of performance and on helping the employee succeed. Since the feedback is ongoing, formal evaluations should hold no surprises.

OBJECTIVE
V.
SUBJECTIVE

It's important to focus your evaluations on information rather than opinion. Metrics often play a role in this (e.g., the percentage of people who received required safety training this year), but information about the behaviors observed or reported is also important (e.g., when I walk through the plant, what do I see?)

Effective managers gather information through monitoring in addition to the use of metrics. Their data sources are interpersonal as well as technical. By regularly observing what an employee does, asking the employee for updates, and talking to others with whom the employee interacts, a manager gains a good appreciation for the individual's performance and can gather specific behavioral examples for discussion with the employee. Examples of behaviors to reinforce as well as behaviors to modify are important for the manager to deliver specific and actionable feedback to the subordinate.

Set and apply clear consequences

The final component of accountability is the use of consequences to support and drive behavior. Effective consequences are clear, well understood, and consistently applied, both positive and negative, for performance relative to safety goals. There are a variety of consequences that can be applied depending on the organization. For example, salary increases and bonuses can be impacted (positively or negatively) for managers' and supervisors' performance. Awards can be given. Progressive discipline can be used. Regardless of the consequences chosen, they must be applied consistently.

Among the possible consequences for poor performance is discipline. As discussed in chapters 13 and 14, a properly designed and implemented discipline system is a valid and appropriate component of any safety system. However, proper design and implementation requires transparency of expectations and consequences as well as consistency in application. A discipline system should never be used solely in reaction to injuries.

SHARED RESPONSIBILITY

Having clarity within the organization about who is responsible and accountable for safety is an important, foundational step toward building strong performance. Once responsibility is clearly understood and accountability established, managers can address issues such as setting goals, creating life-saving rules, enforcing rules, and leveraging the safety resources. The remaining chapters in this section address these topics.

CHAPTER NINE
THE ROLE OF THE SAFETY PROFESSIONAL

In my job, I am a safety resource, not the safety cop.
—SAFETY PROFESSIONAL AT A PETROCHEMICAL COMPANY.

Safety professionals have long been the focal point of an organization's environmental, health, and safety (EHS) performance. Even as methodologies evolve, new tools emerge, and thinking changes, organizations—and managers—continue to count on the safety professional to guide the core of EHS functioning and provide direction on safety strategy. Whatever their area of expertise, be it industrial hygienist, safety, loss prevention, or any of a myriad of other areas, the safety professional's core duty is guiding the organization in the prevention of exposures that cause harm to people, property, or the environment. Safety professionals are an important ally to managers. Learning how to partner with safety professionals effectively is an important part of managing safety well.

A ROLE IN MOTION

Effective partnerships are built on clear expectations. So what is the purpose of a safety professional, and where does this role fit with respect to others in the organization? Like safety itself, the answer the role of the safety professional has evolved over time.

When an organization is just beginning to address safety, it is not uncommon for people to believe that safety outcomes are the responsibility of the safety professional—an approach that cannot work since no staff function can control what happens day-to-day in the line organization.

Most organizations have come to recognize that the safety professional is in a staff (rather than line) role and is there to provide support to the line managers who must "make safety happen." Leading organizations also recognize that the safety professional should play a broader role as a change agent.

Safety today is increasingly treated as a function integrated with the fabric of the business, having tangible business impacts, rather than as a discrete function managed by a handful of specialists. More organizations are expecting safety thinking and engagement from employees across levels and functions—from executives to the front line. Organizations are also recognizing that a wider scope of systems outside traditional safety programs influence safety functioning.

These developments, while undoubtedly positive, pose a challenge to both the organization and its safety professionals. Simply put, a wider role for safety in the organization will mean an increased need for strategy and change management expertise among safety professionals, and an increased demand for complex information about exposures and the factors that create them. For even the best safety professionals, being pegged as a "technical expert" without strategic capabilities can increasingly limit options and opportunities—and ultimately the ability to shape safety functioning within the business. For managers, this creates the need to select and develop safety professionals differently than has been the historic norm.

DEVELOPING SAFETY PROFESSIONALS AS CHANGE AGENTS

While technical knowledge is important in a safety professional, managers should be looking for their safety professionals to be effective change agents. A change agent is in the business of advancing performance by identifying how to get to a newly desired state and enlisting others in that endeavor. Change agents in safety do not leave their technical expertise behind; they simply leverage it to develop strategies for sustainable, high-level performance. The difference between technical expert and change agent here is that the technical expert is solely concerned with the contents of safety programs and initiatives while the change agent is also concerned with how to ensure adoption of the overall safety strategy in a way that will produce sustained performance.

There are a number of elements that create effective change agents: remaining ever curious, continuously learning, building fluency in the behavioral sciences, and understanding organizational dynamics and consequence management. At its core, the competencies of an effective change agent come down to three things: knowing and maintaining focus on the safety objective, understanding behavior, and understanding culture and safety climate.

Knowing the focus

The focus of a technical expert tends to be on the particulars: What hazards exist where and what systems are needed to mitigate them? A change agent needs to develop a view of the performance target that is high and broad. The ultimate goal of any safety effort is to reduce exposures. However, managers should expect their safety professionals to go beyond concentrating only on finding and removing exposures. Charge your safety professionals with adopting a high and broad focus that looks for how exposures are created by organizational systems and the interactions of people with technology and processes.

Organizations striving to achieve safety excellence need this view in order to identify previously unknown or underappreciated exposures and assure that the mechanisms they install are effective at controlling exposures. By providing this view, the safety professional helps your organization move away from "chasing injuries" and toward integrating risk management within the business itself.

Understanding behavior

Safety professionals are often drawn into discussions about behavior, namely how do we get people to do the right things in the right way? From an on-the-ground perspective the solution to a safety-related behavior—for example, employees not intervening when they see a peer working at risk—might seem to be simple. Develop a check list, put people in a training session, and tell them we expect them to do it. This might work if the only barrier to the behavior was a lack of awareness or feedback skills. However a change agent will want to know exactly what factors are driving this behavior in order to create the right solution. This is the kind of advice that managers want to encourage from their safety professionals.

A very helpful tool that managers now expect safety professionals to understand and use is behavior analysis (often called ABC Analysis), a method that helps decipher what influences organizational behavior. This technique is described in chapter 4, and helps us to understand (and ultimately modify) the influences on the current behavior. When you are able to dig in to what shapes a behavior, you gain a better understanding of how to change it.

Understanding culture and safety climate

Change agents are sensitive to the cultural factors that shape outcomes. Culture here refers to the shared values and beliefs of an organization that create the normative behaviors found within the organization. Climate is the prevailing influences on a particular area of functioning (such as safety) at a particular time. One can think of culture as background influence on the organization, while climate is foreground.

Climate changes faster than culture, often very quickly after a significant incident. Without significant and conscious effort, however, the underlying culture is likely not to change sufficiently to prevent further incidents. As the saying goes, "When strategy meets culture, culture always wins." Culture is a creation of leadership. To become an effective change agent, the safety professional must understand the ways in which managers are shaping culture (through their behaviors, decisions, and influence styles) and what effect that is creating on safety functioning. As a change agent, safety professionals must alert you as the manager when you are taking the short view, challenge a strategy that is not going to deliver sustainable improvement, and provide sound recommendations for how to proceed.

While the safety professional has traditionally been expected to possess technical knowledge, the safety professional as change agent requires additional skills. Safety professionals in the future will be expected to understand the principles of organizational change management so that they can help design initiatives that succeed in the short- and long-term. They will need to understand business so that they can make meaningful contributions to strategic-level discussions. They will need to be able to communicate with business leaders in business terms. And they will need to be effective in collaborating and partnering with managers to advocate the safety agenda.

PUTTING THE PIECES TOGETHER

Transitioning from technical expert to change agent does not happen overnight; the competencies outlined here take study, practice, and persistence. While there will always be a need for technical expertise, seeking out and developing safety professionals who can be effective change agents will position them to be valuable assets to your organization, enhance their professional satisfaction, and ultimately help your organization to better protect lives and livelihoods.

CHAPTER TEN
ESTABLISHING SAFETY GOALS FOR MANAGERS AND SUPERVISORS

True motivation comes from achievement, personal development, job satisfaction, and recognition.
—FREDERICK HERZBERG

Managers provide the first line of defense in managing safety issues, communicating organizational priorities and values, and building relationships with individual team members. They act as messengers from the senior leader to the employee—and back up to leadership. Not surprisingly, being a manager is challenging under the best of circumstances. You have multiple priorities but limited time in which to manage them. Engaging supervisors and managers effectively in safety requires more than a general charge to "support safety." Organizations need to define specific activities both that can be integrated with the supervisor's or manager's other tasks and demands, and also that support safety performance effectively.

communicator

A HISTORY OF GOOD INTENTIONS

In many organizations it is common practice to hold supervisors and managers accountable for safety by including a safety goal in the individual's annual performance goals or objectives. Where this is done, the widespread approach is to give each individual an injury rate goal for his department or group.

This is not a good approach for several reasons:

1. Unless the group is large, the random variation in injury rate will be far larger than the real improvement or degradation of safety in any one year.

2. Goals provide an antecedent that prompt behaviors. When bonuses or salary raises are based on injury rate, achievement of the target rate results in a strong consequence for behavior. The behaviors that have most direct "line of sight" connection to an injury rate goal are a set of behaviors that focus on managing the number, not taking steps to reduce exposure and improve safety. For example, a manager may be prompted to focus strongly on return to work programs, or may, intentionally or not, convey to workers that minor injuries should not be reported, or may be tempted to push the envelope on whether or not something is considered reportable. None of those actions have any impact on whether people get hurt.

3. The cultural message we send is that we care about statistics, not people. Employees are more likely to support organizational objectives and take initiative when they feel valued by the organization. Reducing safety to a numbers-focused issue undermines this.

Organizations recognizing the issues with using injury rate for individual goals often see that a better approach is to establish safety goals related to the preventive programs that the organization wishes to emphasize. However we frequently see that when this approach is attempted, the goals established are vague, not aligned across the organization, and/or not relevant to the individual manager or supervisor.

HOW TO SET EFFECTIVE GOALS

Strong, meaningful safety goals and objectives for individual managers and supervisors can be set if a few principles are followed:

Begin with a vision

What activities and initiatives will be used in the coming year to identify and control safety exposures? These may or may not differ for different parts of the organization, but for each manager/supervisor's area of responsibility they should be something that is relevant to the activities of the area.

Identify the actions involved

Understand what the individual manager/supervisor should do to make the target exposure control initiatives effective and successful. This means not only that there is activity, but that the activity is effective. For example, it is not sufficient to say that a manager should perform weekly walk-around safety inspections. Rather, we should think about the desired outcome from those walk-around inspections.

Be sure the goal is level appropriate

First-level supervisors' goals are likely to involve interaction with front-line workers and the use of safety systems. Senior executives' goals are more likely to involve monitoring the performance of other managers and communicating priorities. In every case, the goal needs to reflect where the individual can have greatest impact on making exposure-reduction efforts effective.

Express the goal in specific, concrete, measurable terms

In our walk-around inspection example, we might decide the right goal is for the manager to conduct weekly safety walk-around inspections during each of which the manager engages with at least two hourly employees, provides feedback on some observed safety practice (using an effective feedback model such as the CAR/AR[1] model), and asks the employee about whether they are aware of any safety issues needing attention.

Consider the desired culture

In addition to specific goals, it is important to express the goal in terms that consider the desired culture—that is, both *how* and *what* is to be done. In the example immediately above, including in the goal the expectation that workers will be engaged and feedback will be given in the right way reinforces the culture. If the goal were simply expressed as "do a weekly inspection," that cultural reinforcement might or might not occur.

Establish the tracking mechanism

How will you track and measure performance against the goal? You may elect to use a formal record keeping mechanism, periodic check-ins by the individual's manager, or even self-reporting. Regardless what method you choose, it is critical to determine the method at the outset, when the goal is established.

[1] CAR/AR refers to a feedback technique in which positive feedback is delivered using context-action-result and guidance feedback is delivered using context-action-result with the addition of suggesting an alternative action and alternative result.

Check in at regular intervals

Each manager/supervisor's manager needs to check in regularly on progress being made against the goal. If a goal is established and then not ever discussed, it is easy for the person with the goal to conclude that the goal is there simply for "cosmetic" reasons. However if one's boss periodically asks for an update on progress being made, it becomes clear that the goal is important to the organization.

Establish the goal collaboratively

Good goals reflect the mutual objectives of an individual and his boss. This means avoiding the extremes of a goal dictated by one's boss in a vacuum on one end and leaving it up to the individual without other input on the other. An effective safety goal is established based on a discussion between the individual and her boss, both of whom are aware of, and follow, the principles described in this document.

WHAT DO SAFETY GOALS LOOK LIKE?

The following are examples of the types of things that can be incorporated into safety goals. As noted above, the goals that are appropriate vary by level of the individual manager and supervisor:

SMART
GOALS

WHO WILL DO WHAT,
BY WHEN + HOW WILL

First-line supervisors

The focus of a supervisor's goals is on providing feedback and assuring that safety systems are functioning. Examples might be:

AUDIENCE
BEHAVIOR
CONDITION
DEGREE

- Discuss safety with front-line employees daily, asking about their perceived highest priority exposures.
- Provide feedback (positive and guidance) at least twice a week to front-line employees using CAR/AR.
- Monitor use of safety procedures and systems.

- Identify and reduce/eliminate one safety exposure per month (or quarter), which includes communicating it well across the division so others can benefit by learning what you did.
- Meet with the behavior-based safety facilitator once per month to ensure he or she is getting active leadership support from you.
- Meet with active observers in your department at least once each month to ensure they are getting active leadership support from you and to learn about which exposures are most frequently seen as at risk in your group
- Enforce safety rules consistently—that is, independently of whether an injury occurred, who the employee is, etc.

[handwritten margin notes: SENTINEL COACH COORDINATOR LEAD HI-PO]

Someone who manages first-line supervisors

The focus for this manager is on performing actions that assure that first-line supervisors are performing their roles vis-à-vis safety. Examples might be:

- Review jobs with the highest safety hazards weekly and discuss with first-line supervisors how exposure is being managed.
- Observe supervisor safety briefings and provide feedback to the supervisor.
- Identify and reduce/eliminate one safety exposure per month (or quarter), which includes communicating it well across the division so others can benefit by learning what you did.
- Meet with the behavior-based safety facilitator once per month to ensure that he or she is getting active leadership support from you and your management team.
- Perform one site audit for a work team outside of your department in collaboration with that department's manager to provide a "fresh look" and provide feedback to peer managers.

Someone who manages managers

The focus here is on modeling safety leadership behaviors that are desired throughout the organization. Examples might be:

- Incorporate safety into various (specified) types of communications.
- Ask about safety during all operational meetings and during site visits and facilitate sharing of experience among groups.
- Ask for periodic briefings on safety/injury-prevention programs from managers reporting to you.

CHAPTER ELEVEN

THE NON-OPERATIONS MANAGER:
An Underused Safety Resource

> *We must make safety personal at every level of the organization.*
> —VICE PRESIDENT, OIL & GAS ORGANIZATION

In many organizations when the topic turns to safety, non-operations managers—those in finance, communications, marketing and sales, and even sometimes human resources and law—see this as time to sit back. Non-operations managers often don't see a strong connection between their roles in the organization and the improvement of safety. If that attitude is accepted, the organization makes a big mistake.

WHY SHOULD NON-OPERATIONS LEADERS BE INTERESTED IN SAFETY?

While the connection of operations managers to safety may be more readily apparent, non-operational managers also have an interest in, and involvement with, safety for a number of important reasons.

When safety excellence is an organizational objective, it needs to be supported by everyone in a leadership position. In accepting the role as a leader, regardless of functional area, a manager accepts collective responsibility for the health and well-being of everyone in the organization. It is not "optional" or "role-dependent"; it is an integral responsibility of management.

Beyond the general responsibility for advancing organizational objectives, non-operational leaders often have responsibilities that involve operations—for example a procurement function within finance may include materials handling in the stockroom. These leaders need to speak the same language and have the same expectations regarding safety as their operational colleagues.

Even if they do not have line-of-sight operational responsibility it is likely that the people reporting to non-operational managers have some level of exposure to safety hazards. For example, these workers may be exposed to driving safety risks (e.g., as outside sales people) or to repetitive trauma ergonomics injuries (e.g., as office workers doing large amounts of computer work.) Non-operational managers need to recognize that even if their people do not use wrenches or work on assembly lines, there is still exposure and the potential for injury.

In addition, organizations have an interest in developing their people, and it is not unusual for someone who begins in a non-operations role to find herself transferred or promoted into a role where operations responsibility is part of the job. Taking steps to be involved and learning to be an effective manager of safety makes one a more well-rounded manager, adding value for both the organization and the individual.

HOW DO NON-OPERATIONS MANAGERS INFLUENCE/IMPACT SAFETY?

While operational managers may have a greater degree of responsibility for implementing the safety management and technical systems, non-operational managers generally have responsibility for the organizational sustaining systems—those systems that provide consequences and in so doing indicate organizational priorities and values. Examples of sustaining systems are the performance management/performance evaluation system, the system for selecting promotion recipients, and the systems for awards and recognition.

There are several things that non-operations managers should do to contribute to safety excellence.

When non-operational managers talk about safety they can have a strong impact. The fact that this topic is perceived as being outside of the immediate responsibility of these managers makes their attention to it a strong message about the pervasiveness of safety as an organizational value.

To better enable themselves to understand and talk about safety, non-operational managers who do not have a clear understanding about exposure and what that looks like should take steps to learn. They can do this by partnering with someone in operations to walk through operations and develop a better picture about safety-critical behaviors and practices and what the common barriers to safety are for employees.

Non-operational managers should ask their internal customers what they do to drive safety excellence and how the non-operational manager and his or her function could support those activities. Examples of ways in which non-operational managers can support the safety efforts of operations include:

Communications professionals

Help assure that safety is integrated into the various mechanisms used to communicate within the organization, and that safety messaging is effective and well delivered.

Finance managers

Ask if safety has been considered in capital projects and other types of expenditures. While they most likely will not be able to assess the adequacy of what is being included for safety, they can ask how safety considerations were arrived at, how they can be assured these considerations are adequate, and how the budget for these things was arrived at.

Human resources managers

Ask if safety performance has been considered when someone is recommended for promotion and whether they can assure that when promotions are made the announcement highlights the individual's contributions to supporting corporate values, including safety.

Non-operations managers

Participate in hazard analyses and incident investigations. While these individuals may lack the technical expertise typically sought for hazard analysis and incident investigation, their participation can bring unbiased eyes to the issues. This can contribute to better outcomes, strengthen the knowledge and commitment of non-operational managers, and send a strong cultural message about the value the organization has for safety.

CONTRIBUTING TO SAFETY EXCELLENCE

Safety excellence is best achieved when there is broadly based support and participation among managers, including those whose responsibility does not include operations. Taking steps to encourage safety participation by non-operations managers engages a resource that is often overlooked.

CHAPTER TWELVE

LIFE-SAVING SAFETY RULES:
Effective Implementation

If we can't keep the promise to our people that we will keep them safe, what promise can we keep?
—METALS COMPANY EXECUTIVE

There are some situations and tasks so hazardous that approaching them unsafely just one time can result in a serious or fatal injury. "Life-saving rules" (sometimes known as cardinal rules) are designed just for these situations. These rules are deemed to be safety-critical and there is zero tolerance for violation. Adoption of life-saving rules can be a helpful approach to ensure ongoing focus on those protective measures most important for avoiding serious injuries. That doesn't mean, however, that implementing them is easy. Without a carefully planned approach, implementing life-saving rules, rather than protecting employees, can result in serious problems that actually detract from an organization's safety objectives.

WHY ARE LIFE-SAVING RULES SO HARD?

The principle of life-saving rules is straightforward enough: Some situations are inviolable in their seriousness and there can be no deviation in approaching these situations with utmost care. So why is it that so many organizations find that these rules can become points of contention, or worse, inconsistently used? Before we look at how to implement life-saving rules well, it is helpful to understand the pitfalls that managers can fall into with respect to them:

Inconsistent enforcement

A life-saving rule must be enforced with 100% consistency based on the rule being followed, independent of whether there is an injury that occurs. Still, one of the most common ways that an organization can undermine the rules is to allow variation in how life-saving rules are enforced.

Solution

The organization must be prepared to commit to 100% enforcement and must be prepared to discipline anyone, whether agreement worker or supervisor or manager, who does not follow the life-saving rule. In addition, a supervisor or manager who does not enforce a life-saving rule with consistency must be disciplined. (That is, zero tolerance applies both to following and to enforcing the rule.) Additional discussion of the proper use of discipline is found in chapters 13 and 14.

Unclear consequences

Say there is a life-saving rule around following the confined-space entry procedure. That procedure may require display of the completed work permit in a visible location close to the work being performed. The person doing the work takes appropriate precautions, completes the permit perfectly, but puts it in his pocket. What action do you take? Without clear guidance and communication, some managers would interpret this as a rule violation and apply discipline, while others would say the procedure is designed to control exposure for the most high-risk activities and the failure to post doesn't warrant discipline.

Solution

There must be clear consequences for failure to follow a life-saving rule. This may already be specified in various labor agreements and/or HR policies, but the consequences need to be reviewed to be sure they can be applied with 100% consistency of enforcement.

Moreover, it is important to define what "zero tolerance" really means. As a team, walk through as many types of potential scenarios as possible, so that you can agree on the desired approach and communicate it clearly.

Lack of specificity

Having a life-saving rule of "act safely" (or something similarly ambiguous) is impossible to enforce consistently. The definition admits too much room for interpretation.

Solution

Assure that each life-saving rule is specific enough to support alignment. Instead of "act safely," you could define what that means in specific circumstances, for example, "No work between or under rail cars without blue flag protection."

Poor selection of life-saving rules

Sometimes life-saving rules are drafted in response to issues that are important but that don't meet the qualification of being life-threatening. For example, attempting to address late reporting of injuries through a life-saving rule would potentially create two problems: First, it would make the life-saving rules appear to employees not to be focused on reducing exposure. Second, it could be seen by regulators as suppressing the reporting of injuries (since some injuries truly cannot be reported until sometime later and subjecting this to discipline could result in people not reporting legitimate injuries).

Solution

Select life-saving rules for their ability to reduce high-risk exposure, not for administrative issues.

HOW TO SAVE A LIFE

So how do you avoid the pitfalls and go about establishing effective life-saving rules?

Describe the compelling reason for change

Change starts with a vision. Fundamentally, you want senior leadership to articulate why this change is important and what benefits we will achieve through the change. Questions to answer might include: Why are we making this change now? What will the change look like?

Form a cross-functional implementation team

This team's purpose is to manage the development and implementation of life-saving rules. (Ideally this team is a joint management/labor team.) Implementing a life-saving rules program is a significant undertaking and requires considerable planning and development work. Having participation and input from varying perspectives is important to assure the program and implementation itself are both well designed.

Make an initial selection of life-saving rules

Aim to identify a small number of rules, ideally no more than eight or ten, that represent high risk in your organization. You may select rules based on their reflection of exposures with very high-severity potential or because they reflect exposures with lower severity but very high frequency. The credibility of the life-saving rules depends on them being items that everyone would recognize as important for worker protection. (It should be apparent to everyone that they would not want to be working with someone who violated these rules.) Study of the injuries with potential for serious injury or fatality can be a good source of data to support development of life-saving rules. In addition to identifying the life-saving rules, it is important to decide on two related issues:

1. *Will life-saving rules be enterprise-wide or department specific?* In other words, are the exposures in different departments sufficiently unique to require separate life-saving rules, and if so how will these be applied in locations where more than one department's personnel work?

2. *Do we need to eliminate variation in existing procedures before we can implement life-saving rules?* For example, there may be multiple versions of lock out/ tag out procedures within the organization. Unless these are made consistent, a life-saving rule that said "follow lock-out/tag-out procedures" would be very difficult to validate (see below) and consistently enforce.

Define the consequences

There must be clear and unambiguous definition of the consequences that will occur when a life-saving rule is violated. Because these rules must be enforced with 100% consistency, the organization must define consequences that it is willing to truly use. Of course these consequences must be consistent with any requirements or restrictions contained in labor agreements. The consequences may be progressive— that is, a different consequence for first offense than for subsequent violations—but the consequence at each step of progression must be applied consistency to anyone violating a life-saving rule.

Union collaboration

In organizations with labor unions, there should be early communication with the union leadership about the organization's reasons for implementing life-saving rules, the principles under which it is being done, and the approach planned to implement it. Input should be sought on both the draft rules and the implementation process so that hopefully the unions can support this endeavor, but if they are not willing to actively support it, at least they do not try to block it.

Validate life-saving rules

You must assure that if rules are going to be enforced with zero tolerance for violation that the rules can, in fact, be followed. For example, in some organizations we see a rule requiring tie-off for people working at heights, but people are assigned jobs in situations where there is nothing to which they can tie off. Every life-saving rule must require a behavior that is enabled. Rules should be validated by having them reviewed by employees who do the work in which the rules apply as these employees will best understand what barriers may exist to following the rules.

Communication to employees

There must be a well-designed communication plan that reaches all affected employees and explains why this change is being made, what the life-saving rules are and why these specific things were selected, how the rules were validated, and what consequences will occur in case of violation of life-saving rules. The plan should provide multilevel ongoing communication covering not only the compelling reasons for implementing life-saving rules but also what each level's (senior leaders, mid-managers, front-line supervisor, and front-line worker) roles are, and what they need to do to make the process successful. A "one and done" communication approach will not be sufficient.

Train supervisors and managers

All supervisors and managers must be trained to understand how to recognize life-saving rule violations and how to handle these violations. The training should involve both classroom and field training prior to implementation of the life-saving rules. For agreement workers, before going live with life-saving rules it is valuable to create "teachable moments" where no repercussions exist. This helps ensure both the supervisors and the front-line workers understand what is expected and what good looks like. This may be done through an initial "grace period" during which life-saving rule violations will result in correction but not discipline.

Provide methods for barrier removal

Even when you have tried to assure that a life-saving rule will always be enabled, there may be situations that are missed in which there is a physical or systems barrier preventing the rule from being followed. It is important that workers have a reliable mechanism to report any situation they know of or encounter where a life-saving rule will not be able to be followed. This mechanism should also provide feedback to the worker on how the situation is being addressed.

Pause work authority

If there is zero tolerance for violation of a life-saving rule, then workers must be allowed to refuse work that can't be done other than by violating a life-saving rule, and that refusal must have no adverse consequences for the worker. (In fact, a worker refusing to violate a life-saving rule should get positive feedback for doing so as this presumably avoided a high-risk situation.)

Monitor enforcement

Implement a process to monitor the performance of supervisors and managers in enforcing the life-saving rules.

LEADING THE WAY

Regardless of whatever else is happening, good managers know that they must never lose sight of the fundamentals. In safety, those fundamentals include a focus on life-altering injuries. You need not be a safety expert to assure the appropriate use of life-saving rules. You only need an acquaintance with their principles and an unflagging attention to their use.

CHAPTER THIRTEEN

WHEN TO USE DISCIPLINE:
Principles for Getting it Right

A coach is someone who can give correction without causing resentment.
—JOHN WOODEN

Discipline is among the most confusing and controversial topics in safety. On one hand, it is obvious that companies must have safety procedures and rules. And once those rules are established, it is crucial to support and enforce them. Managers know—as company attorneys routinely remind them—that if they know about a safety rule violation and they ignore it, they put themselves at risk. On the other hand, the punitive aspect of disciplinary programs seems to undermine the kind of workplace collaboration and participation essential to success in productivity, quality, and safety. The topic becomes even more delicate when an injury does occur.

There are two aspects to the discipline question: When and how. Both must be thought through and carried out in an effective discipline system. In this chapter we discuss when to use discipline, and in the next chapter we discuss how.

THE DISCIPLINE DILEMMA
An employee has just suffered an injury. Preliminary findings show that the employee failed to follow written procedures and the injury was a direct result of this failure. Now one senior leader is pushing for disciplining the employee, and you need to make a decision about how to proceed. Is discipline the right thing to do here?

For some, the answer is clear from the preliminary findings: The employee should be disciplined *because* he failed to follow a written procedure. For others the description we've revealed so far provides far too little information; they want to know things such as:

1. How seriously was the employee injured?
2. What is the employee's history relative to safety compliance?
3. Was this a willful violation?
4. Did the person violate the spirit of the procedure or the intent?
5. What influence did leadership or the employee's peers have in the decision to violate the procedure?
6. How was the employee trained and/or informed about the procedure?
7. Were there extenuating circumstances that made following the procedure undesirable, impossible, or even unsafe?
8. What systems are in place to assure ongoing compliance? What data is available regarding monitoring this procedure and levels of compliance?

One could ask why any of these questions are relevant. How would the answers influence the decision? The bottom line is that the employee did not follow a written procedure.

UNDERSTANDING DISCIPLINE

Before we can define the rules around when to discipline, it is essential to understand the purpose of discipline in safety and its role in an overall system for injury prevention. The discipline system is a mechanism for providing clarity around organizational standards and what the organization values. It is also a mechanism for providing corrective consequences to those individuals who do not live up to these standards and values.

When it comes to managing exposure and influencing behavior, discipline is the last line of defense; it indicates failure in the systems designed to control exposure. When discipline is routinely required to control behavior, then one really needs to consider what failures have occurred in the overall system. The failures could be related to hiring decisions, leadership capabilities, or competing rewards systems. Seldom can an organization "discipline its way" to better performance or an improved culture; yet in an organization where there are no real or perceived adverse consequences for unwanted behaviors it is a good bet that the number of undesired behaviors will rise, not decrease, and the result will be poor overall functioning and high rates of injury and people abusing the system.

The most important consideration in using discipline is that the decision to administer discipline has to be fair and just. These decisions must be consistent, evenhanded, and based on transparent criteria. When a decision to discipline is seen to be unjust, it has huge negative implications to the culture, relationships, and on whether future incidents will be reported.

How do you know if your organization needs to review its use of safety-related discipline? Here are a few warning signs:

1. Incident investigation typically stops when at-risk behavior is found. There is no push to understand what influenced the employee to make this choice.
2. Incident investigations frequently result in punishment for the employee, unless an obvious unsafe condition contributed to event.
3. The primary action items coming from an investigation are: writing a new rule or procedure, retraining, threatening people around compliance, or offering trinkets to raise awareness.
4. The numbers of non-lost time or medical treatment cases are equal or less than the number of lost time cases. This indicates that employees are likely hiding injuries to avoid being disciplined since we normally see more non-lost time than lost-time injuries.

FOCUSING ON THE ESSENTIALS

Given that discipline is a valuable tool, but with significant downside potential when misused, how do organizations begin to evaluate its use in their own approach to safety? Discipline works best when it is used consistently and the rules around its application are fair and well understood. The following principles, derived from our work with organizations around the world, provide a helpful starting point for governing your decisions around when to administer discipline as it relates to safety.

Principle 1: *Decide on what is crucial and treat those things accordingly*

For almost every organization there are a few infractions where there absolutely has to be zero tolerance for variation. In these instances, management needs to clearly define and communicate what these infractions are and communicate why these items are being handled uniquely. Managers must also assure that these behaviors are within the employee's ability to perform.

Many organizations call these life-saving rules. These are the rules that result in the most severe form of punishment if a person is found in violation, which often means termination. Life-saving rules apply to that small set of rules or procedures where 100% compliance is necessary because there is a much higher potential that the outcome of violation will be a life-altering event or fatality. Some examples are things such as:

1. Smoking in process areas where flammable materials are present.
2. Failure to de-energize and isolate equipment before working on it.
3. Texting while driving.
4. Working on railroad track without authority.

Implementing life-saving rules must be done with care, and the issues involved are discussed in Chapter 11 of this book.

Principle 2: *Do not determine discipline based on the fact someone was injured*

When employees perceive that discipline only happens in the aftermath of an injury, there is a very real risk that future incidents, no matter what the level of potential, will go unreported. Effectively, we're telling employees that punishment and reporting are always connected.

How do you determine whether or not discipline is tied to injuries? Look at the total number of times discipline for safety was administered and look at the percentage of the total that directly followed the employee being injured. A percentage over 50% strongly suggests that employees will perceive they are being disciplined for being injured, not for the infraction that led to the injury. Also look at incident investigations and see how often the only actions identified are formal discipline or other employee-focused actions (new rules, retraining, etc.) that are perceived as negative by the employee. There are two main reasons that organizations can inadvertently find themselves in a situation where discipline becomes virtually synonymous with reporting:

Haphazard Safety Management

In today's "more with less" organization, supervisors and managers are more office bound than ever before. They are conducting fewer and fewer safety audits, observations, and other field activities. Often, the only time a manager finds out about a safety infraction will be when an incident happens and he needs to investigate. It's not surprising, then, that the investigation system would end up being used as a substitute for regular field verification. Ultimately, this is a poor compensating approach that can backfire into a major event—a fatality or life-altering injury—that appears "suddenly" with no apparent warning signs. The data that would have suggested the potential for such an event went undetected .

Lack of Support

Organizations can also inadvertently undermine the discipline system when they ignore the consequences that discourage supervisors from using it as intended. A supervisor attempting to administer discipline may find herself having to defend her decision in a grievance hearing, or may have to do considerable paperwork, or may find that her manager routinely overturns her decision. If the consequences to the supervisor encourage overlooking violations and not using the discipline policy as intended, then this will occur until there is an event that simply can't be overlooked. Organizations often fail to understand the consequences driving supervisor behavior and assuring these consequences are aligned with desired performance.

Principle 3: *Avoid increasing severity of discipline simply as the result of a reported incident*

Most discipline policies apply counseling or coaching rather than a more punitive consequence to a first offense. Don't ignore this policy simply because an injury occurred. If an employee is hurt and the employee violated a rule or procedure and this is the very first time this employee was found to have violated the rule or procedure, do not depart from the normal first step of progressive discipline.

If the employee had been coached, counseled, or disciplined for the same offense previously and this latest incident resulted from a repeat of that same offense, then the next step in the discipline process should be followed.

A GOOD FOUNDATION

An effective discipline system establishes a clear set of rules and applies them consistently. That sounds simple enough. But as we've seen, assuring the consistency means providing managers with the necessary support to attend to safety needs regularly, not just when it is in crisis. With a good foundation, managers can begin the work of refining the practice of discipline itself.

CHAPTER FOURTEEN
HOW TO USE DISCIPLINE:
Principles for Getting it Right

You don't lead by hitting people over the head.
—DWIGHT D. EISENHOWER

In the previous chapter we discussed when to use discipline in connection with safety issues. In this chapter we discuss the other element of discipline: How to use discipline. As in the case of when to use discipline, there are a number of principles that can be applied to thinking about how to use discipline.

THE ART OF CORRECTION

Discipline serves as the last line of defense in managing exposure and influencing behavior. To be successful, a manager who must discipline an employee must be clear and decisive. At the same time, he or she must be sensitive to applying discipline at the appropriate times and with the right intent. When we don't consider the effect that discipline has on people, we undermine the integrity of the discipline process and in turn that of our exposure control systems. We also create negative effects in the culture that linger long after the disciplinary action itself.

The "how" of an effective approach to discipline comes down to achieving the delicate balance between rigor and flexibility. We don't compromise on the principles and timing while at the same time we seek always to apply the rules fairly and with the good of all employees in mind. These practices come down to five principles concerning causation, procedural justice, transparency, feedback, and maintaining discipline in the right perspective.

Principle 1: *Keep an open mind on causation*

What leaders believe about the underlying causes of mistakes subtly, but powerfully, influences how leaders approach safety-related performance. There are several theories and beliefs that you may hear thrown around about human error. For example:

- Workers are only responsible for 15% of mistakes where the system implemented by management is responsible for 85% of the unintended consequences (W. R. Deming).
- 88% of accidents are the result of unsafe behavior, 10% by unsafe conditions, 2 % unavoidable (H.W. Heinrich).
- Some people are just predisposed to getting injured.
- Impairment, especially that related to drugs and alcohol, is a major factor in accidents.

One of the worst things a leader can do with respect to safety is to bring such preconceived ideas to the disciplinary process. Attribution bias can skew our ability to accurately interpret causation. Attribution bias is the unconscious tendency we all have to understand one's own success in terms of personal powers and abilities while seeing one's failings as the result of bad luck or external, situational causes. Attribution bias leads us to believe when someone outside our peer group (particularly if it is someone we don't like) is involved in a car accident, it's probably because he is a bad driver, while if *I* get into a car accident, it's because the roads were slippery. In the workplace, attribution bias can lead us to assume that an injured person was at fault and we are inclined to believe that the cause of the incident was the person's behavior, lack of motivation, or even lack of intelligence. On the other hand, when we are personally involved or the person involved is a peer, we tend to assume that the cause was an outside factor, such as inadequate training or direction, not being given enough time, inadequate equipment or systems, or the actions of others.

Attribution bias can lead us to focus on one aspect of causation and miss the bigger picture. This is especially acute in an organization whose culture is to assign blame rather than to seek out root causes. Management tends to assume the employee is the problem and employees focus on leadership or system problems not only because it is their natural bias but also as a defense mechanism, and any discipline that results is perceived as unfair. Overcoming attribution bias and developing a complete understanding of root causes helps to make any discipline that results from an incident feel more just.

Principle 2: *Understand procedural justice and consider it in applying discipline*

Procedural justice has to do with fairness and transparency of the method used to make decisions that impact an employee. Employees from organizations that score high on procedural justice will make comments such as, "The decision making process is free of bias," and "If I have a concern about a decision that is made that I think was unfair, I can always go talk to my supervisor, his boss, or the Human Resources department."

Procedural justice determines whether an employee who gets an outcome that was not in her favor walks away unhappy or angry. An employee who receives an unfavorable outcome but believes the decision-making process was procedurally just is disappointed. However the employee who receives an undesired outcome and believes the process used to get to that decision involved favoritism and bias will be understandably angry. If perceived procedural justice is low there is a much lower likelihood that the disciplined employee will learn from the experience and change behavior: The discipline will ultimately be ineffective.

There are two important Procedural Justice issues when it comes to making the decision about punishing for a safety violation. First, no organization, no matter how close to perfection they are, can write a rule or policy that covers every known contingency and is appropriate 100% of the time. There are times that varying from a policy makes sense. However when this occurs, it is important for the reasons to be transparent and consistently applied or the variation will undermine perceptions of fairness.

Second, front-line leaders feel pressure to protect their most reliable and hardest working employees. They may be tempted to overlook things in these employees that they do not overlook in others. When it comes to applying discipline, making a decision not to discipline because "he's a good employee" must be avoided.

Principle 3: *Regularly review your policy on disciplining safety violations, explain how the system works, and explain why the system is designed the way it is*

Things change quickly in organizations. Leaders move on, procedures are updated, rules are rewritten, employees join and leave the workforce. Routine leadership team reviews of the discipline policy, optimally once a year, allow the organization to assure that the system is still aligned with reality on the ground. In addition to discussing issues that might suggest a policy modification, routine reviews also allow leaders to assure that new employees have been appropriately onboarded with respect to the discipline policy and that they received the message intended. It is common to see organizations where new employees and new leaders were not told about crucial policies. Onboarding communication can also become less effective over time; at times when there is pressure to reduce training time or to introduce new training technology, we can inadvertently eliminate the opportunity for people to ask clarifying questions.

Principle 4: *Avoid the "focus on failure" trap*

Discipline is an effective tool when employees see that it is one part of a balanced system. Most employees follow the rules, most of the time. So in a balanced system, the majority of the feedback they receive would be for doing the right thing. In an unbalanced system, however, the feedback skews toward one aspect of performance. When an organization only addresses at-risk behavior through progressive discipline, employees would only (or largely) receive feedback when they did something wrong. The result is that people learn to "hide from leadership." The more unbalanced the feedback system, the more employees will avoid reporting incidents, even those with high potential.

The best way to achieve balance in the feedback system is for supervisors and managers to get into the field and monitor performance. This puts the focus on performance, not failure. It tells employees that we place a high value on safety and compliance. And it puts the leader in a position to routinely recognize good performance and identify variation before there is an adverse event.

Safety can be more challenging to monitor than other performance areas because to understand what is really happening we need to monitor compliance in a wide variety of settings, day shift and night, during normal operations and when there are unusual levels of production, etc. It's only human nature that if a leader walks the location at 2 p.m. every Friday to monitor, employees will adapt to the leader's schedule. Leaders who want to see what is really happening and position themselves to provide meaningful, balanced feedback, vary the time and location of their monitoring.

Principle 5: Don't rely on discipline as the main tool in fixing a broken safety climate

There are times when the safety climate and behavioral reliability (in terms of safe behaviors) have degraded to a point where leadership decides to do something drastic to regain control before someone gets seriously injured. The most important thing to remember is that the employees are not to blame for the situation. They are operating within the structure, systems, and culture that leadership has allowed. So moving from the current state to a new, desired future state takes more than firing an employee to make a statement. It is necessary to bring about fundamental change in expectations about safe behaviors and the consequences for not following them. So how do you respond it a situation like this?

- First, take a deep breath (because we know you want to jump into action) and visualize the desired future state for handling procedure or rule violations.
- Write down your thoughts in behavioral terms: What specific actions would you see people doing in your desired future culture?
- Put into words why this change is important to you, the organization, and the employees.
- Discuss your thoughts with your leadership team and listen to their reaction and concerns.
- At this point consider involving other key leaders in the organization. If you are working in a unionized site, inform the union leadership as early in the process as possible.
- Do a gap analysis to figure out what needs to happen to achieve this change.
- Develop a communication strategy that will assure every employee is informed of the change and why the change is happening.

One group that must be given special consideration is front-line leadership. Supervisors are likely the ones who will have to change the most. Frequently they are the ones who see most of the variation and violations, and they have to decide on how to handle each situation. Given the normal variation in capabilities and skills, there can be wide variation in how the same violation is handled. One leader will want to proceed with firing the rules violator and the next will want to pull the person to the side and coach them and implore them to comply. This variation in how the situation is handled is likely to cause additional problems in the organization, and so front-line leaders' reaction to variation and violations must be calibrated and made consistent.

During this time of change it will be important for senior leadership to be in the field coaching and mentoring the front-line leaders. This will likely be a drastic change for the front-line leadership group, and they need to know that senior management appreciates the difficulties they face and will back them up.

PUTTING DISCIPLINE IN PERSPECTIVE

So do the questions we posed at the beginning of the prior chapter matter when an employee violates a written procedure? In reality you can misapply or properly discipline with or without considering those factors. If the design and application of your discipline system is not properly in place before the employee violates the rule, it's likely that you have already compromised your ability to have the decision perceived as fair and just.

Most employees follow the rules and comply with the safety requirements most of the time. While discipline is a necessary tool to get the attention of a few, it is one of the least effective for handling the majority of employees. As you think about applying discipline for safety violations, consider whether your approach is balanced (meaning the majority of feedback employees get about safety-related behavior is positive) and fair. A safety program without a discipline component is incomplete, but a safety program with a poor discipline component is ineffective.

CHAPTER FIFTEEN

SAFETY STAFFING:
Who, Where, and How Many

We needed employees to understand
we were flying people, not planes.
—PIERRE BEAUDOIN, PRESIDENT AND CEO BOMBARDIER

We are often asked by organizations how many safety staff people they should have. Having a simple guideline (e.g., you need one safety person for every X employees) would certainly make it easier for organizations to evaluate the adequacy of their resources and plan for the future. Unfortunately, there is no one-size-fits-all formula. Differences in organizational structure, work processes, culture, and exposure profiles require differing levels of support and expertise for mitigating exposure. Managers responsible for staffing safety functions must instead evaluate the unique needs of their teams to determine whether the resources provided are adequate for the work that is being performed.

WHAT DETERMINES STAFFING NEEDS?

An organization's set of safety resources reflects its own unique configuration of exposures, people, and processes. There are different safety roles and responsibilities to consider. There are also types of specialized expertise that must be available. Exactly what is required, how much is required, and how to provide it depend on a number of factors.

Type of exposures

The primary role of any safety resource is to reduce exposure. What those exposures are (and consequently the type of resource we need to address them) change depending on a number of factors, including:

- Work tasks performed
- Conditions under which tasks are performed
- Variability of the tasks
- Materials used
- Age and condition of equipment
- Technologies employed
- Extent of contractor use
- Degree of independence in the work (e.g., distributed workforces or high worker-to-supervisor ratios)
- Amount of automation

Safety involvement of non-safety employees

What roles and responsibilities for safety are actively performed by people in non-safety roles (such as operations, maintenance, engineering, front-line workers)?

Compliance needs

Regulatory compliance can vary in complexity depending on:

- Number of countries in which operations occur
- Intricacy of applicable regulations
- Scope within which "safety" is defined—e.g., is process safety or nuclear safety included, is security included, is workers compensation management included?

Safety expertise

What are the regulatory/legal requirements for safety staff in the regions where we operate?

BUILDING THE RIGHT TEAM: TWO KEY CONSIDERATIONS

A strategic approach to safety staffing considers the nature of exposures, the organizational structure most appropriate to addressing those exposures, and the competencies required for individual success. Fundamentally, there are two areas that organizations must consider in developing the right approach to staffing: organizational structure and the safety staff itself.

Organizational structure

The optimal organizational structure for safety management has long been a subject of debate. Should safety decision making be centralized to one person or body or spread out? Should staff report to operations or outside of operations? At what organizational level should safety leadership reside? Again there is not one "right" answer. The organizational structure for safety is best considered a dynamic arrangement, dependent on both the organizational philosophy and the state of its evolution in EHS.

There are several guiding principles to consider:

- The organizational structure used for safety needs to be consistent with the overall organizational philosophy of the organization. In other words, in an organization that is highly decentralized, safety will be more effective if it is decentralized, while a highly centralized organization would be best served by a strongly centralized safety function.
- If the organization requires a high degree of consistency in implementation of safety systems and processes, a centrally managed, field-based organization may be most appropriate.
- An organization must reach a certain level of maturity in safety before line management leaders truly grasp

and exercise the responsibility for safety. When that has happened the safety function needs to be configured to support them. But until that occurs, it may be more appropriate to have a strong central safety function that can help the organization move toward a greater degree of maturity in safety.

• All organizations need some level of central review, control, and resource to ensure that corporate policy, practice, and learning are managed according to both the organization's strategy and proven best practice.

Safety staff

In general, line management should be responsible for implementing the safety system and for safety performance. But line managers need support from a resource (individual or group) with deep technical knowledge, strong knowledge of laws and regulations, and the ability to provide strategic guidance to line management regarding the overall safety system.

The safety staff function is typically charged with:

• Advising senior leadership
• Establishing policies and standards
• Providing periodic audit assurance of the performance of operations
• Providing safety expertise and guidance to operations (where safety expertise, in advanced organizations, includes guidance on leadership and culture as well as technical aspects of safety).
• Providing leadership of incident investigations and data analysis and ensuring outcomes are communicated and embedded across the wider organization

In more advanced safety functions we are also seeing a bias toward safety staff providing coaching and guidance to leaders in the field, in their natural work environments.

The organization and reporting relationships need to support the safety professionals' ability to fulfill these roles. It is common for there to be a group or subgroup that provides policy and audit functions and a different group or subgroup that provides guidance and expertise. These may be different departments (e.g., a corporate department and operating unit) or may be different groups within the same department.

With an understanding of safety experts' roles, there are several other considerations for supporting this resource.

Safety Talent Management

Traditionally, the safety professional role was a largely technical one, and the key qualification was technical knowledge, supported by skills in training and general interpersonal skills. That role is changing. Looking ahead, the most effective safety personnel will be those who can be effective change agents in their organizations. While technical knowledge will still be required, there will also be a need for safety personnel to understand behavioral principles, culture, leadership, and organizational change, and they will need competence in influencing, communication, and coaching others as well as in data analysis and program development and evaluation.

Developing Safety Leaders

In order to drive safety as strategy, an organization's leaders must develop a deep understanding of, and appreciation for, safety. At the same time, few safety leaders have developed exclusively through the safety route. Rather, they have learned safety, operations, and leadership expertise across a wide variety of roles outside the safety function during their careers. An effective safety resource plan provides exposure to safety issues for leaders within and outside explicit safety roles.

STAFFING FOR SUCCESS

The right amount and configuration of safety resources will vary with the maturity of the organization's safety effort and will likely change over time.[1] As an organization becomes more mature in safety, the involvement of non-safety personnel in safety activities increases. This often results in the need for fewer dedicated safety personnel.

---

[1] For a comprehensive discussion of the evolution and stages of maturity in safety see *The Zero Index*, Colin Duncan, general editor, (Ojai: Safety in Action Press, 2012).

MONITORING PERFORMANCE

One of a manager's key roles is monitoring performance and making adjustments as necessary to meet objectives. This is no less true in safety. This section addresses the accountability function of monitoring and providing feedback on performance as well as several topics related to overall monitoring of organizational performance through metrics and through more hands-on approaches.

CHAPTER SIXTEEN
METRICS:
Looking Forward and Backward

Without the right data,
you don't know what you don't know.
—Transportation industry executive

All managers require metrics in order to make decisions about resources, strategy, and direction. The right set of measures in safety helps us understand risk and performance. An incomplete set of metrics, on the other hand, can skew our perception of risk and endanger our ability to lead safety well.

TYPES OF INDICATORS

Safety is one of the few performance areas in which most organizations across a wide variety of industries use a common metric. This is the medical case injury rate,[1] most often defined as number of cases per 200,000 hours worked, is sometimes supplemented by a lost workday case rate and/or a severity rate (number of lost workdays per 200,000 hours worked). *TRIR*

While it is helpful to have a metric that allows us to compare across industries, companies, facilities, and departments, most organizations find themselves relying almost exclusively on these lagging indicators as safety performance measures. And as managers have understood since the wave of Total Quality Management (TQM) thinking swept the U.S. more than 25 years ago, effective management requires leading as well as lagging measures.

[1] Also known as the total recordable rate, and in the U.S., as the OSHA recordable rate.

Lagging metrics quantify what has happened. Leading metrics provide an indication of what is likely to occur in the future. Leading metrics in safety provide information with which a manager can intervene in advance of injuries occurring.

Metrics are usually described as being either leading or lagging. A more granular approach to defining a safety scorecard, however, identifies four categories of metrics that provide a comprehensive picture of safety performance.

Two of these categories are different types of leading indicators:

Exposure metrics

These measure exposure and changes to exposure. Tracking changes in exposure metrics provides indication of when underlying aspects of the operation are creating increased (or decreased) likelihood of a safety incident.

Control metrics

These measure the effectiveness of exposure mitigation measures and when the use or performance of those mitigation measures indicate increased or decreased likelihood of a safety incident.

Measuring the two types of leading indicators provides management with "early warning" on the need to increase scrutiny or intervene to assure that risk levels do not increase.

Lagging indicators

Defined as metrics reflecting what has already happened, these metrics make up the third category. Injury rate is a lagging indicator as it reports the number of injuries that have occurred.

Precursor events

The fourth category of metric sits in between the leading and lagging indicators, and reflects precursors events that can result in fatalities and serious injuries. We describe this as sitting between leading and lagging because these metrics reflect things that have occurred, but uses those as leading indicators of the potential for future incidents with more severe outcomes.

Separately tracking the potential for fatalities and serious injuries is important because potential for these is not necessarily controlled through the programs that address safety overall. Managers who understand the potential for fatality and serious injury can make conscious decisions about targeting and prioritizing safety efforts. Serious and fatal injury prevention is discussed further in chapter 17.

LEVERAGING LEADING INDICATORS

There is no perfect suite of measures common to all organizations. Each organization needs to aim for a set of measures that provides useful and robust indicators of how it is doing against its objectives. The upstream nature of leading indicators mean that they often need special attention in determining which make the most sense for your organization.

Types of control metrics

Control metrics are most often used for accountability, and provide data to help managers assure that the intended activities are being done. Accountability measures are a means of motivating people to perform. They relate to specific performance expectations and specific people. The idea of accountability measures is not new, and accountability through "management by objectives" type systems has been common practice in industry for decades. However these metrics are rarely direct predictors of future injury. A few examples of control metrics are:

Inspections planned vs. completed

This measure tracks the number of inspections, including safety committee and supervisory walk-arounds, completed compared to the number planned. The metric is reported as number versus plan and as percentage of plan completed.

Open safety work orders > 60 days

This metric tracks the number of open items in the work order system that are designated as safety items and that have been open for >60 days. Items will include actions arising from both inspections and audits as well as employee-raised issues.

Leadership audits

This metric tracks the number of field audits/inspections/walk-arounds done by a location's senior leadership team members per team member during the quarter.

Mechanical integrity testing % past due

This metric shows the percent (%) of scheduled mechanical integrity tests overdue for key equipment, including: pressure vessels, tanks, piping (visual and thickness test), relief systems, and instrumentation.

Types of Exposure Metrics

Exposure metrics tell us how successful we are in achieving our ultimate objective: Lower exposure directly correlates with fewer injuries. Examples of metrics that are direct indicators of level of exposure include:

Number of safe work permit jobs

This measure tracks the number of tasks for which safe work permits are required during the month. Jobs requiring safe work permits are, by definition, higher risk. Therefore an increase in the number of these jobs is indicative of a higher exposure profile.

Newer workers

This measure can be defined as the number of workers who performed work for which they had less than one-year experience during the last month. It is generally known that workers are most likely to be injured and make errors during their first year, so growth in the number of newer workers is indicative of increased exposure in both personal and process safety.

Process excursions/upsets

This measure is defined as the number of times during the month that any process has a parameter that falls outside the "not to exceed" limits for the process. Even when exceeded limits are managed without adverse outcome, their occurrence is indicative of exposure increase. Any change in number or pattern of process upsets should be cause for increased attention.

Percent safe behaviors

The percentage of behaviors observed to be done safely can be an indicator of exposure, provided that the observation process is specifically designed and implemented to produce "measurement quality" behavioral data.[2] This means that the behaviors being observed are accurately reflective of the exposure profile in the work, that the observation strategy produces a valid representation of the work, that inter-observer consistency is assured, and that there are clear decision rules for classifying what is observed.

As exposure and control metrics are developed, it is important to assure that the measures correlate with outcomes, and that the data-collection process supports production of valid, consistent data. A well-designed set of safety metrics will help managers monitor performance and make appropriate interventions to prevent injuries.

Each organization should develop its own set of leading indicators and precursors of serious injuries. Experience shows that the leading metrics that will be meaningful vary from company to company and for different types of operation.

THE BIG PICTURE

A thorough approach to safety measurement would involve appropriate use of exposure metrics, control metrics, serious injury/fatality precursor event metrics, and downstream or outcome metrics.

---

[2] Note that few behavior-based safety processes are designed to meet these criteria

It is important for managers using safety performance measures to understand what each metric means; safety professionals need to assure that their management develops this understanding.

CHAPTER SEVENTEEN
PREVENTING FATALITIES AND LIFE-ALTERING INJURIES

Treating all exposures equally, while well intended, doesn't make sense when roughly 80% of injuries represent low-severity potential.
—THOMAS R. KRAUSE

Serious injury and fatality (SIF) prevention has long been considered a matter of numbers. Reduce "smaller" events, the thinking goes, and you will also reduce more serious ones. This conventional wisdom has not served leaders well. Serious injury events continue to plague otherwise strong safety performers. Data show that while industry has made tremendous strides in reducing less serious injuries over the past 20 years, the rate of fatal injuries has remained relatively flat. Understanding the reasons behind this discrepancy—and knowing the principles for addressing them—is critical to your success as a safety leader.

THE RELATIONSHIP BETWEEN MINOR INJURIES AND FATALITIES
The Heinrich Triangle has been a fundamental concept in workplace personal safety for many decades. This model simply says that the frequency of injuries goes down as severity goes up—i.e., there are more medical treatment cases than lost-time cases, and more lost-time cases than fatalities. The Heinrich Triangle has been interpreted

by the safety community as telling us that if we reduce the number of less severe injuries, we will reduce the number of more severe injuries as well—shrink the bottom of the triangle and you shrink the top.

However, national data in the U.S. over the past 10 years shows medical treatment injuries steadily declining, but fatalities remaining essentially level (see Figure 17-1).

Occupational Fatalities and Non fatalities

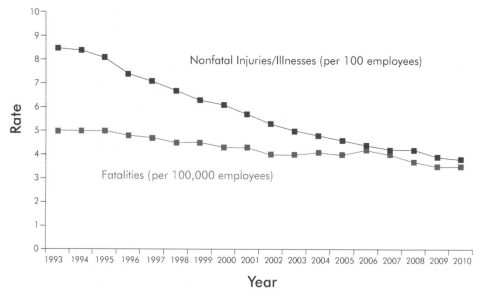

Figure 17-1. Source: United States Department of Labor, Bureau of Labor Statistics, 2011.

These results are inconsistent with how the Heinrich Triangle has been interpreted and raises questions about its validity and the validity of prevention efforts.

Research undertaken in 2011 helped explain the apparent contradiction between experience and theory and provides important lessons for managers concerned with prevention of fatalities and serious injuries.

The research confirmed that:

- There is an inverse correlation between frequency and severity of injuries. Less severe injuries do occur more frequently than more severe injuries.
- Reducing the number of incidents at the bottom of the triangle does not necessarily reduce the number at the top in a proportional way.

The potential for a fatality or serious injury is highly variable across the types of less serious injuries that occur, reflecting the fact that serious injury or fatality (SIF) potential varies among different types of exposure. (For example, a back strain from lifting a load has little SIF potential, while a fall from an elevated work position has high SIF potential.) As a result, a particular safety initiative may be highly effective in reducing the number of injuries with low SIF potential, while having little or no impact on the exposures with high SIF potential.

We also know that specific types of work activities and safety controls are most closely associated with incidents that have SIF potential. For example, injuries involving equipment and pipe opening of hazardous chemicals, lock out/tag out, machine guarding and barricades, confined space entry, and use of hot work permits tend to have SIF potential, as do operation of mobile equipment, water craft, working under suspended loads, and working at elevations. Examining the exposures for a specific company or location can identify those with high SIF potential, allowing the design of interventions that focus on those exposures.

SIFS ARE NOT FLUKE OCCURRENCES

It is not uncommon for managers to react to fatalities or life-altering injuries by suggesting that the incident was a fluke and not indicative of a broader safety issue. This is flawed thinking.

The occurrence of a major event requires a specific and infrequent configuration of factors—a variety of conditions must occur and the safety controls designed to protect against injury must fail. A series of things all must occur, and each of these things individually has a low probability. A machine must malfunction requiring maintenance, the lockout of energy is done incorrectly, the supervisor fails to catch the error, the machine cycles unexpectedly, and someone is in position to be injured. The chances that the first and only time a machine malfunctions that the lockout is done incorrectly, and no one notices, and the supervisor doesn't catch the problem, and an individual is in position to be injured when the machine cycles is low. It is much more likely that breakdowns have occurred often, and lockout is not done rigorously, and lockout jobs are not carefully checked, so that eventually one of these events will cause a serious injury, but the underlying exposure has occurred many times before and gone unrecognized.

It is important to understand the fallacy of the "fluke occurrence" idea. If SIFs truly were fluke occurrences, then there would be little chance of preventing them. However because they are not, but rather the product of conditions and behaviors that have occurred previously, it is possible to detect exposures with SIF potential and mitigate the exposures.

CONSIDERATIONS FOR REDUCING SIFS

While many organizations are aware of non-SIFs that have high potential, few have the consistent visibility needed to address precursors in sustainable ways. Since medical case rate changes are not indicative of changes to SIF potential, in the absence of measuring incidents with SIF potential organizations have no way to assess whether they are making progress in reducing the exposures that contribute to SIFs.

In designing interventions to address SIFs, the following principles should be followed:

- Educate people at all levels on the difference between general injury prevention and SIF prevention.

- Track SIF potentials as a separate outcome metric, combining actual serious injuries and fatalities with less serious injuries that have SIF potential.
- Develop interventions to reduce SIFs that are not one-time activities, but part of an ongoing process. These interventions need to engage employees at all levels, use data analysis to understand sources of precursors, and provide sustainable mechanisms to identify and address precursors.
- Use targeted mechanisms to identify and address precursors. Most precursors can be identified through a system that combines effective observation with focused discussion/interviewing in the workplace. Implementation of this process should occur within a change management framework.
- Both the design of safety systems targeting SIFs (their integrity) and the quality of how they are implemented (conformance) should be addressed.

IMPLICATIONS

One cannot assume that just because overall injury rates are declining that the likelihood of a fatal or life-altering injury is also declining. These most serious injuries result from an identifiable subset of all exposures. Managers need to seek to understand these exposures, regularly review data on the frequency of incidents with serious outcome potential, and implement targeted exposure mitigation efforts aimed at these exposures.

CHAPTER EIGHTEEN
TRUST AND VERIFY:
Audits and inspections

*Safety is not an intellectual exercise to keep us in
work. It is a matter of life and death.*
—BRIAN APPLETON, TECHNICAL ASSESSOR
TO THE PUBLIC ENQUIRY OF PIPER ALPHA

Most safety programs include one or more types of audit among their
key activities. How well audits contribute to safety depends directly on
how the audit program is designed, implemented, and supported. Audit
programs are not the mechanism to enforce good safety practice (that is
the role of discipline, as described in chapters 13 and 14); rather they are
a mechanism to assure that performance matches intent. There should be
a presumption that people do the right things to assure safety. However,
even with that presumption there is value to periodically verifying
that programs are implemented as intended through an audit process.
Managers play a key role in assuring that audit activities are effective.

WHAT DO WE MEAN BY AUDIT?
A definition of terms is necessary before beginning a discussion of
audits. The word "audit" has been applied loosely and at various
times has been used to describe all of the following activities:

Compliance verification
Audits are often done to confirm compliance with regulatory requirements and/or company rules and policies. These audits are often
done using teams from outside of the area or facility being audited.

Housekeeping and conditions inspections

Periodic evaluations of housekeeping conditions and/or the condition of facilities and equipment are sometimes referred to as audits (as in "housekeeping audit"). This type of review is typically done within a department or facility, by a manager, a safety committee, or a safety professional.

Behavioral observation

At times behavioral observations are referred to as audits. This is usually a misnomer as the way behavioral observations are generally scheduled and performed does not provide information that can be generalized to conclusions about a facility or workgroup.

Hazard identification walk-around workplace inspections to identify hazards are sometimes referred to as audits. This is a similar activity to housekeeping and condition audits, but tends to look more deeply to identify hazards that are not adequately controlled.

Audits are one of those safety activities that are sometimes done without a clear vision of the objective. When this happens the activity can become institutionalized without there being any way to evaluate its effectiveness. Managers responsible for the audit process as well as managers whose operations are being audited should be clear about the purpose of the audit program. An audit program may have any one or more of the following objectives:

- SCORING FOR COMPARISON OR TRENDING—Some audits produce a numerical score that can be used to rate a location or department, compare it to others, and trend performance over time. While a popular approach, this tends to make the exercise about the score rather than about safety improvement. Audit report-out meetings focused on negotiating to get a better score compromise the value of the process.

- ASSURING REGULATORY COMPLIANCE—Audit programs that are initiated from corporate staffs often have the objective of providing assurance to senior executives (and sometimes to the board of directors) that the organization is complying with regulations. While this is an understandable objective, it is limited in its impact on actual safety performance. As discussed in chapter 7, regulatory compliance in safety does not provide assurance of good performance.

- IDENTIFYING ISSUES THAT COMPROMISE EFFECTIVENESS OF SAFETY SYSTEMS AND THEREBY INCREASE LEVELS OF EXPOSURE—An effective audit program will identify weaknesses in the safety systems before incidents occur. This often requires looking beyond regulations and checklists, and understanding how the systems should work and how they are implemented on a day-to-day basis.

An audit program may address any one or any combination of these objectives. Audits that focus on objectives one and two tend to be infrequent events that happen on a set schedule. They often involve an outside entity. These types of audits are valuable to determine where the organization is at risk from a governance standpoint. Audits that primarily target the third objective, such as life-saving procedure audits and key process audits, occur routinely and are a part of the standard work for management, supervisors, engineers, and safety professionals, with high-functioning organizations engaging front-line workers in the effort. These routine audits are crucial for reducing the potential for catastrophic events, including fatalities and life-altering injuries and other incidents.

THE MANAGER'S ROLE

Managers responsible for audit programs, whose operations are being audited, and who receive audit results, all have key roles in making an audit program successful and effective. A manager's roles include the following:

Align participants on the objectives

Be sure that you and everyone involved as an auditor or an "auditee" is clear about the objectives of the audit and its importance. The most effective audit programs occur in a collaborative environment in which everyone recognizes the opportunity to confirm the effectiveness of safety programs and identify improvement opportunities. The least effective audit programs become adversarial, with the group being audited perceiving the need to prevent the auditors from finding things. If the objective is understood to be making safety programs as good as they can be, and the consequences of adverse audit findings are to focus on improvement rather than focusing on blame and punishment, then the audit program can be truly effective.

Contribute to process selection

Make sure you understand the audit process. The way in which audit information is gathered and evaluated directly influences the results and their reliability. Some audits involve only examining records to compare documentation to what is expected. That approach will not reliably uncover situations where the actual conditions or activities are inconsistent with the paperwork. Other audits involve only observation of the operation and the work. In that case the auditor's opinion is based solely on what happens to be occurring during the audit, and that may not be representative of overall operations. A third approach is to gather information through individual and/or group interviews. This approach may provide perceptions rather than evidence-based information. The best approach to auditing it to use a combination of all three—documentation, observation, and interviews. How the audit uses these approaches and how data from each approach is evaluated helps a manager judge the validity and generality of the audit findings.

Guide the selection and use of criteria

Understand the audit criteria—that is, the benchmark against which audit information is judged. If the audit findings are based solely on the judgment of the auditor (or audit team) without criteria, then there is likely to be significant variability in audit findings among audited locations. For this reason virtually all audit programs have a set of criteria against which audit evidence is assessed. If the audit criterion is compliance with regulations, then the audit will have limited value in helping you achieve excellent performance, for the reasons discussed in the chapter 7. If the audit criteria are regulations and company standards and policies, the findings are likely to be more helpful, but are still limited to identifying issues in those areas for which there are standards. Some audit programs supplement findings based on company and site standards with a separate section in which the auditors point out general observations. These observations are typically based on the judgment and experience of the auditor, and so are subjective and open to discussion, and are not treated as audit findings (which typically must be addressed), but rather as suggestions for areas that local management should consider.

Enable an effective process

Provide the resources (generally time) needed for a high-quality audit program. In addition to giving qualified auditors the time to do an effective job, the audited site will be spending time helping auditors review documents and procedures, making employees available for interviews and site tours, and providing general support. If the managers of the location being audited recognize the value of an outside look, they will appreciate this as time well spent.

Follow through

Perhaps the most important aspect of an audit is what happens after its completion. An audit will usually identify some areas for attention. Management must have a system for assigning accountability for resolving audit findings, monitoring completion of these actions, and documenting the actions taken. Audit findings that remain unresolved represent uncorrected exposure situations and also increase liability.

Communicate audit findings. Any time an audit occurs, you can be sure that it will be widely known within the operation. Sharing audit results, as well as plans for addressing any audit findings, demonstrates your concern for safety and commitment to improvement. It also provides an opportunity for front-line workers and first-level supervisors to provide additional information that can be useful in understanding why audit exceptions occurred and how to address the issues.

Get perspective

Audit findings are much more than a list of tasks to be completed. Take the opportunity to take a broader view and ask why these issues arose in the first place. Just as we should look for root causes in the case of an injury, we should also seek to understand the root causes of management-systems breakdowns. If an audit finds that inspection of fire protection systems is overdue, inspecting the fire-protection systems may resolve the immediate issue. But if the underlying reason is that fire-protection systems are not included in the preventive maintenance scheduling system, then the problem is likely to be repeated unless the root cause is identified. Audit findings are your prompts to look for systems issues that might otherwise be invisible.

CONSIDERATIONS

Audits can provide valuable information. They also bring fresh eyes to the evaluation of safety in an operation. However audits can cost more in terms of resources needed and distractions created than the value they deliver in safety improvement. Whether an audit produces value commensurate with its cost depends to a great extent on how managers help to structure and implement it. By understanding the characteristics that make an audit program effective, managers can assure that this activity contributes to superior safety performance.

MAINTAINING ALIGNMENT

Managing safety is about more than watching the numbers. Achieving consistently excellent performance in safety requires the active engagement of everyone in the organization, with consistent communication and reinforcement in ways that convey the importance of safety.

This section addresses the value and importance of feedback as a tool in your safety arsenal, how to achieve real engagement in safety, and how to be an effective safety communicator without inadvertently sending the wrong message.

CHAPTER NINETEEN

THE ROLE OF FEEDBACK

*If the first time I have presented a constructive criticism
to a subordinate is in his or her year-end review,
then I have screwed up.*
——ROBERT STEVEN KAPLAN,
CO-AUTHOR OF *THE BALANCED SCORECARD*

Feedback is one of the pillars of performance management. While
culture may establish the shared values that frame my work, it's the
direct communication of feedback that tells me how I, as an individual, align with organizational values and expectations. Managers
adept at feedback are better able to influence behavior, redirect performance, build understanding of organizational objectives, and
demonstrate leadership. Despite its importance, many managers find
feedback a difficult practice to master and end up underusing it or
doing it in a way that is ineffective.

COACHING

WHY FEEDBACK WORKS

Simply speaking, feedback is information about performance in rela-
tion to a specific, accepted goal. Feedback is a consequence, which
means that it motivates behavior. (See chapter 4.) People who are well-
informed about their performance are better positioned to make decisions and choices about how they behave in the workplace. A less well
appreciated, but equally significant aspect of feedback is that it influences the self-attributions of the person who receives it. This means
that it impacts how he thinks and feels about himself. For example,
hearing from you—the boss—that you see me as someone who is
always willing to learn something new helps me to think of myself as

the kind of person who can take on new challenges; it might give me the confidence I need to stretch myself that extra little bit.

Feedback also provides the manager a way to give—and gather—information about performance in a way that is more immediate, direct, and powerful than downstream outcomes. For example, discussing a supervisor's strengths and opportunities after she just conducted a safety meeting is more helpful to her than interpreting results of a general employee survey six months to a year later. With feedback, the supervisor has the opportunity to leverage and improve her behaviors now. Without it, the supervisor relies on her own perceptions of how the meeting went, and very likely will continue to do what she has always done.

COMMON MISCONCEPTIONS

For all the benefits of feedback and recognition, many managers and supervisors hold misconceptions that prevent them from taking full advantage of this best practice. Understanding the common reasons that feedback is underused helps us to recognize how to use feedback more effectively.

I already do feedback

An infrequent conversation about performance is not feedback unless it provides information that is meaningful to the person receiving it. Performance reviews are often a good example of "non-feedback." The review may tell me that I succeeded or failed—which in most cases I already know—but seldom does it give me the information I need to change my performance. Feedback is essentially developmental; a report card is not.

Frequency is not always a measure of effectiveness. I can have frequent interactions that lack substantive content. The manager who regularly tells her reports "good job" without indicating specifically what is being recognized is not giving feedback effectively. Feedback is information about performance relative to a goal. Unless the performance and the goal are communicated, you are not really providing feedback.

Feedback is only for low performers

Managers will often say, "Feedback is a nice thing for other people to be doing, but my team doesn't need it." A related idea is that, "If one of my team needs feedback on their performance, I'll get someone who doesn't." In reality, feedback is essential to improving the performance of any team, no matter how good they are. It is a rare manager who would honestly say that he doesn't expect his reports to improve their performance. When managers miss the opportunity to gather and deliver information about performance, they send the message that they're satisfied with the status quo—a message no forward-thinking manager wants to send—and they fail in their responsibility to develop the capacity of their team.

Feedback takes too much time

Managers are already busy people, and adding activities may seem unrealistic. However, feedback and recognition done well can be naturally folded into a manager's day. Managers and supervisors are already interacting with their reports in informal interactions, meetings, e-mails, and so forth. Adding a few moments to ask how the employee is performing on a certain project and providing feedback takes little time, but greatly enhances the quality of the manager's relationship with that employee and the likelihood that the employee will meet or exceed goals.

Feedback is micromanaging

Some managers feel they are micromanaging when they provide feedback. In particular, the monitoring that accompanies feedback can be perceived as taking away from the employee's discretion in doing his or her job. However skillful monitoring and feedback does just the opposite; it enables the employee to perform better and gain new confidence in their decisions and actions with the manager's support. Good managers don't want to take over the jobs of others; they recognize that their job is to be interested in what their reports are doing and to help them perform optimally.

Feedback should "happen naturally"

It's a common myth that feedback can only be effective for the talented few managers who are good with people or who enjoy a natural rapport with their reports. Nothing could be further from the truth. Usually, this perception comes from experience with the kind of feedback that is not well-grounded in monitoring performance (that is, the feedback has little information to give). As you would expect, such feedback results in discussions that seem insignificant or shallow. Effective feedback is a skill that can be learned and is a practice that must be planned for to be leveraged successfully. This doesn't mean it needs to be time consuming. It just means that improving his reports' performance needs to be on the manager's radar screen. It will then be actively woven into the fabric of already existing interactions.

GETTING FEEDBACK RIGHT

Effective feedback starts with the right foundation. One of the reasons feedback may not feel natural is that it lacks an established framework. Monitoring (the gathering of information about performance that provides the substance of feedback) and feedback itself presuppose a context. The organization's objectives provide a framework for monitoring the activities of reports and an anchor from which to give feedback. For example, objectives might include encouraging upward communication about safety or having supervisors respond promptly to safety concerns. Within this context, conversations about safety or response to safety concerns do come naturally.

In addition to establishing a contextual foundation, the manager needs to create a system for gathering the information that supports feedback. Within a workgroup or management team, such information can be obtained through monitoring via direct observation, self-reporting, or review of documentation. In order to gather information about performance lower down in the organization, the manager may need to engage others in capturing and passing along information about front-line performance, including information about individuals deserving of special recognition.

At its most basic, effective feedback includes two elements: success feedback (to reinforce behaviors you want to see continued), and guidance feedback (to redirect those behaviors that need to change). In addition, it is helpful at the outset to establish an expectation with direct reports that they will be providing feedback within a certain context (meetings, one-on-one, etc.) for a certain purpose (furthering safety and organizational goals), and that the employee is expected to be an active participant and contributor to the discussion.

With established mechanisms for monitoring to support feedback and an expectation that feedback will occur, the following principles contribute to effective feedback:

Apply feedback in a timely way

Aim to provide feedback frequently, at consistent intervals, and as quickly as possible following the demonstrated behavior. Saving feedback for the midyear or annual review diminishes its effectiveness as a development tool and reduces the active participation of employees in identifying and improving their own performance.

Make feedback explicit

The best feedback is interactive, with the employee receiving the feedback contributing to the discussion. Be explicit when feedback is occurring; this prevents a misinterpretation of the purpose of the discussion.

Make it personal

To be meaningful, feedback needs to be delivered in a way that communicates the implications of behaviors to the person, the organization, and to you as a manager. State why the behaviors are important and show a genuine interest in the success of the person receiving the feedback.

Use descriptive language

Feedback that is specific and descriptive increases the objectivity and value of performance improvement. This means you should use accurate examples rather than generalizations. The direct report understands exactly what is being asked of him. Using behavioral words to describe what the person did or said is particularly helpful in feedback. For instance saying, "You showed a lot of initiative in resolving that safety issue," is more powerful and likely to be remembered than, "You did a great job."

Leverage self-attributions

One of the most often missed opportunities in delivering feedback is using it to shape self-attributions. Self-attributions are the beliefs that people hold about who they are. These beliefs strongly influence how they perform. A person who defines himself as "someone who always delivers," or the workgroup that describes itself as "a team that works well together," tends to live up to the description. Managers can leverage this in success feedback with comments such as, "I can always count on you to keep a project moving," or "You're the kind of workgroup that pulls together. I always know that I can expect great things."

AN ONGOING PRACTICE

Feedback is a powerful tool through which a manager demonstrates support, reinforces values, and builds accountability. Rather than an infrequent event, feedback needs to be an ongoing practice supported by shared expectations and effective monitoring.

CHAPTER TWENTY

SAFETY COMMUNICATIONS:
Optimizing the Message

The single biggest problem with communication is the illusion that it has occurred.
—GEORGE BERNARD SHAW

[handwritten: COMMUNICATION]

Winston Churchill once remarked that the difference between leadership and management was communication. Safety leaders understand this principle well. They've learned how little great plans matter if you don't effectively articulate the purpose first. Still, many managers find safety communication to be tough going. Despite frequent discussion and meetings among leaders and their reports, we often see good messages get lost in translation, if they are even heard at all. The result is frustration on both sides as safety efforts seem to lack direction and opportunities to improve systems and reduce exposure go untapped. Becoming a better communicator requires attention to two basic things: What you communicate and how you communicate.

[handwritten: START WITH WHY]

WHAT YOU SAY

When it's two o'clock in the morning and there are no managers around, what resonates in your employees' minds as they make safety-critical decisions? It won't be the summary of the latest safety report or a polished speech about the importance of individual responsibility. What employees remember is what they have been told, implicitly or explicitly, about what really matters. This is the goal of communication for a manager: To instill a sense of mission in employees and to create an environment where employees regularly deliver and seek safety-related information.

While the particulars will vary according to your organization and objectives, there are several main topics that all good safety communications cover.

Our goals

Fundamentally, the manager's role is to communicate the safety objectives of the organization and the tactics we will use to achieve them. Frequent discussion of goals, and progress toward the goals, tells employees that safety is important and helps them understand how they can contribute to its success.

The big picture

Instilling a sense of mission means helping people understand what that mission is. In addition to clearly articulating goals, managers also need to help people understand why they matter. See if you can describe the safety goal without referring to numbers, rates, or regulation: You will be describing what safety means to us as an organization.

Our progress

Just as in other areas of performance, managers must continually report back on progress and performance to the group. Where are we improving? Where are we falling behind? What are we doing to address challenges now and down the road? The answers to these and other questions are what employees need to know if they are to keep safety front of mind.

SINEK 131

WHY
HOW
WHAT

HOW YOU SAY IT

What you say is only part of the picture. To be an effective communicator, you also need to consider how you communicate.

Integrate safety into regular communications

Safety is surprisingly relevant to many of the topics that you cover in the normal course of business; as a communicator it's your job to find those moments and reinforce the connection between safety and the business. When you talk about production, talk about safe production. When you talk about expense control, that's a great time to emphasize why we don't sacrifice important areas to realize cost goals. Integrating safety into day-to-day conversations tells employees that safety is an integral part of the way we do business, rather than something set apart (e.g., "Now it's time to talk about safety.")

Focus on the preventive

There's a natural tendency for managers to lean into outcomes (e.g., injury rates) when they talk about safety. The problem with this is that too much focus on what has already happened can foster a sense of blame and even helplessness. Instead, work on communicating with a preventive focus. Emphasize that our goal is to understand and reduce exposure: To look forward. This way you are more likely to be perceived as positive and helpful, and to encourage learning and positive actions.

Balance the big picture with the minutiae

Talking about the vision and long-term goal of safety by itself can leave people unclear on what is expected of them. Talking exclusively about details (last month's injury rate, or a specific safety hazard) can create a sense that safety is purely about meeting short-term objectives. The best safety communicators talk about both: Describing the vision while also relating it to near-term issues and actions that will help achieve the vision.

Make it personal

How you choose to talk about safety can be as important as the contents of the message. Managers who make it personal—conveying a real sense of interest and concern (often based on personal experience)—are compelling and credible. Managers whose safety communication is desultory, impersonal, and obligatory, on the other hand, convey that safety is not a true priority.

Look out for informal opportunities

Communication occurs throughout the day in various ways, both formally and informally. Often the most impactful communications are the informal ones, for example chatting with workers while you walk through the plant. As you go about your day, be prepared to ask specific questions about safety issues—for example, whether there are outstanding equipment issues, or whether workers feel that exposure levels have increased or decreased, or what is their biggest safety concern. You will both convey a real sense that safety is important and learn important things about the working environment.

Emphasize a transformational style

Take the time to explain decisions, actions, changes, and rules, rather than just issuing instructions with the expectation that they will be followed. In this way you help people generalize the principles behind individual decisions and actions. A transformational style builds the understanding, capability, and support necessary for people to act in ways consistent with the organization's intentions—even in the absence of specific guidance and rules.

Emphasize learning over blame

Talking to a worker who has been injured presents a special challenge to managers. There is a need to learn what happened so that the organization can learn from the incident. However, the manager may also feel frustration (especially if the worker violated a procedure or rule). In these situations, remember that the worker involved did not expect to be injured when doing what he or she did. Asking why the worker did something that could cause injury is unlikely to be productive: The worker simply didn't see it that way at the time. A more productive approach is to focus the discussion on exposure. Ask the worker to think about where in the activity preceding the injury that exposure increased. This can help the individual involved learn to assess his work environment more effectively while also exposing lessons for others in the organization.

Pay attention to what you say and don't say

Finally, perhaps the most important and least recognized concept in safety communication is that we communicate through what we don't say as well as through what we do say. When a manager sees a high-risk exposure and elects to say nothing, it sends an important message to the workers involved. When a manager discusses the state of the business or the plans for the coming year or the organization's strategic plans and safety is not included, that speaks volumes about the real value placed on safety by the manager and the organization.

REINFORCING THE MISSION

Done well, safety communication increases safety competence. Not only because it facilitates buy-in and participation, but also because the very nature of safety effectiveness means each employee must understand what the safety issues are and how they are being addressed.

CHAPTER TWENTY-ONE

TRIVIALIZING SAFETY:
Avoiding an Unintended Consequence

If safety is to get a seat at the table, it must be earned.
—OIL COMPANY EXECUTIVE

While most of this book is about what managers should do, this chapter provides some guidance on what not to do.

SIX WAYS TO UNDERMINE SAFETY
Managers and supervisors want to demonstrate their commitment to and concern about safety. Many want to do more than just provide resources and say that safety matters to them. The desire to be a visible supporter of safety is admirable. Unfortunately all too often these leaders take actions that have the unintended effect of demonstrating that they really don't understand safety, or even worse, create the perception that safety is not really taken seriously.

Here are commonly seen ways in which managers unintentionally trivialize safety:

Pay disproportionate attention to minor safety issues
Imagine an organization where people work in high-hazard situations on a daily basis: at elevated heights, with molten metals, in confined spaces, with highly toxic chemicals, and so on. Now imagine that these employees are supported by an office where the most prominent safety signs are the ones telling people not to carry uncovered coffee cups, where every meeting is required to begin with a "safety

minute," and where the featured topic at the last "all hands" meeting was lawn mower safety. These are actual examples. To employees in the field or on the shopfloor—the ones exposed to the most significant hazards—these examples demonstrate that management may mean well but simply doesn't get it. By overemphasizing risks, any risks, the managers in these organizations have instead demonstrated they have little understanding of and appreciation for the full range of exposures employees face every day.

What to do instead

To show concern for safety, you must first understand the risks in the work being done under your span of control. If you are not already familiar with the risks in the work, talk to front-line workers and safety staff, review hazard assessments, and read incident report. All of these will help you understand where people can and do get hurt on the job.

Engage in pro forma performance

When a manager performs safety activities because they are required but lacks real interest or commitment, this is usually apparent to everyone. Most managers understand that they should say something about safety in their communications to subordinates. While few would be so blatant as to spend 15 minutes talking passionately about production and then add as an afterthought, "Oh yes, and let's be safe," many are having the same effect without realizing it. Similarly, a manager or supervisor may be required to do a safety walk-around weekly or monthly, but when that is done from the perspective of "let's get this over with," rather than taking a real interest in understanding what safety issues exist, that tends to be apparent to subordinates. A manager or supervisor who doesn't see value in safety will tend to convey that through minimalist performance of required safety activities.

What to do instead

Challenge your own point of view about what safety is. What you believe shapes what you do—and how you do it. Ask yourself what safety means to you personally (not what you think it should mean, what it really means)—why is it important to you that workers not get hurt? If you have subordinates who lead others, help them develop a personal connection to safety.

Forgive lapses when offset by production

A good, conscientious worker takes a few short cuts with safety procedures to help his group achieve a production target. The worker here is acting in the way he perceives the organization wants, and that belief is likely based on past experience. The dilemma for the supervisor or manager in this situation is that the worker's intentions were good, but the actions were inconsistent with safety. When a leader overlooks the safety lapse because of the worker's intentions, this clearly signals to workers that communication about safety as a value is really just lip service, and safety should be sacrificed when production is at stake.

What to do instead

Apply firm coaching. Acknowledge that the worker may have thought he was doing the right thing. At the same time, clarify that bending the safety rules is not what the organization wants, and if it happens again there will have to be more severe consequences.

Engage people but display lack of understanding

Managers and supervisors are generally encouraged to get out and interact with front-line workers to better understand exposures and to show workers that they are connected and concerned. However doing this without adequate preparation and support can be problematic, especially for a leader who does not have an operations background. A leader who isn't really familiar with how operations work and what demands, constraints, and conditions apply may be perceived as naïve and out of touch.

What to Do Instead
Don't let a lack of operational experience or knowledge discourage you from spending time in the field. Go prepared to learn, for example by touring operations with someone knowledgeable in the activities or by getting thoroughly briefed before visiting a facility.

Appoint weak performers to safety roles
The extent to which safety is important in an organization will be judged in part by the quality of personnel placed in key safety-related roles. In the past there has been a tendency at times for safety roles to be given to individuals who were weak performers in other jobs, or who were "filling out the time" before retirement. When individuals in safety roles do not have the respect of the organization it reflects on the value safety is perceived to have. This applies not only to full-time safety roles (such as safety manager or safety coordinator) but also to part-time roles such as safety committee members.

What to Do Instead
When placing people in safety roles, use the same care and selectivity as you would with the most critical operations management roles.

Fail to demand accountability
When safety roles and responsibilities are assigned and there is no follow-up on performance, it quickly becomes clear to people that the safety assignments are not truly important to the organization.

What to Do Instead
Routinely check on progress and provide feedback on performance against safety-related roles and goals.

AVOIDING PITFALLS

To paraphrase a common saying, the road to under performance in safety is paved with good intentions. A manager or supervisor who understands how good intentions can inadvertently create poor performance will be better equipped to assure that intentions turn into reality.

CHAPTER TWENTY-TWO

EMPLOYEE ENGAGEMENT:
Many Heads are Better than One

None of us is as smart as all of us.
—KEN BLANCHARD

Creating the kind of workplace that embodies safety excellence is a serious undertaking. But there is a limit to the coverage that leaders can personally supply and even the best safety systems are of little use if they aren't followed. Like other critical objectives, safety excellence requires the willing and active participation of employees throughout the organization—particularly of those employees most affected by it. The manager's role is to understand what true engagement is and to foster it among her teams. Engagement is not something that can simply be directed by fiat: It has to be fostered under the guidance of management.

WHY ENGAGEMENT MATTERS

The first step to driving engagement is to understand why it matters. We often hear people talk about the importance of meaningful employee involvement in the safety effort, assuming that everyone understands the reasons for it. It is worthwhile to state why employee engagement is more than "nice to do," and really is vital to achieving safety excellence. Effective employee engagement offers a number of benefits, including:

- A DEEPER BENCH—Instead of relying on safety professionals alone to assure good functioning of the safety systems, we can equip supervisors to be effective safety advocates.

- BROADER RISK DETECTION—Instead of relying on supervisors alone to identify and correct at-risk behaviors, we can enlist all employees in this effort, greatly increasing the number of eyes on the job.

- NEAR REAL-TIME ASSESSMENTS—Instead of relying on an infrequent safety inspection to detect conditions needing correction, we can have all employees on the look out every day.

- A MORE PERSONAL INVESTMENT—Instead of having people feel like safety rules and procedures are a burden being placed upon them, we can have everyone focused on achieving the objective of those rules and procedures—the reduction or elimination of exposure to safety hazards.

- BETTER INFORMATION—Instead of making assumptions about how work is performed and why people do what they do, we tap into the firsthand knowledge of the people doing the work to help us understand where there are high exposures and how to do work tasks more safely and effectively.

CREATING ENGAGEMENT

There are any number of ways to create employee engagement in safety, including approaches that are very effective as well as approaches that fall far short of the goal. The characteristics that help create an effective approach to employee engagement include:

Meaningful responsibility

Employees given the opportunity to take responsibility for a program will usually rise to the occasion, particularly when they are properly supported with effective coaching and adequate resources. On the other hand, employees given trivial "make work" tasks under the guise of engagement will quickly lose interest and become skeptical.

Opportunity for impact

Successful employee engagement occurs when employees feel that they can make a difference. Asking employees for input and not following up on the input received is one of the fastest ways to undermine an employee engagement effort. It is also important that there be opportunity to impact systems and conditions in addition to behavior. Workers recognize that many times an at-risk behavior is the result of systems issues or conditions, and an approach that is limited to worker behavior will be perceived as assuming the worker is always at fault.

Active sponsorship

Employee engagement does not mean management abdication. Whatever ways workers are asked to engage in the safety process, they should be monitored, supported, coached, and held accountable by management sponsors. The objective is to set the initiative up for success, and the experience and influence of managers is an important resource to any employee team.

Broad participation

Having a safety committee with several front-line employees as members may be a useful thing to do, but it is not really a way to achieve employee engagement. Effective engagement provides roles for widespread participation.

Risk-based

Employee participation should reflect a risk-based approach to safety improvement. That is, if employee participation involves only issues perceived as low risk (such as trips and falls in the parking lot) in an organization that has exposure to serious injury potential, there will be little enthusiasm for participation.

Union involvement

In organizations that have organized labor representation, it is important for employee participation and engagement to be done in collaboration with the union leadership. Since improved safety directly benefits union members, there is a confluence of interests between the organization and the union on this issue. However if the union is not involved from the outset, they may see employee engagement as an effort by the company to undermine the union.

ENGAGEMENT FOR FIRST-LEVEL SUPERVISORS

The front-line supervisors (FLS) of an organization are the management representatives closest to the work, and their active and effective participation in safety can make a major impact on the participation of employees. However, in many organizations there is no real clarity about the key safety activities that are needed from FLS and no training provided to assure that the FLS group are equipped to do these activities well.

While this list may be modified or extended to meet the needs of specific organizations and types of operations, in general there are five critical safety functions for first-line supervisors. These are:

1. JOB SAFETY BRIEFINGS—At least daily (and possibly more often depending on the nature of the work) reviewing with front-line employees the exposures involved in the work to be performed and the exposure mitigation measures that should be used.

COMMUNICATE

2. SAFETY CONTACTS—Regularly spending time in the work environment both observing the work and interacting with front-line employees about safety— providing reinforcement for specific safe performance and providing guidance where at-risk behavior is seen.

EVALUATE
COACH

3. VERIFICATION AUDITS—Confirming that safety procedures are followed properly by observing and by checking. For example, when an energy source is locked out, confirming that the equipment being locked out actually has been de-energized (e.g., by attempting to operate it) so as to verify that employees know the procedure and have exercised it properly.

INVESTIGATE
EVALUATE

4. PHYSICAL HAZARD IDENTIFICATION—Periodically inspecting the workplace to identify conditions and equipment that may create exposure and taking steps to get hazardous conditions corrected.

INVESTIGATE
EVALUATE

5. INCIDENT RESPONSE—Handling the immediate and longer-term reaction to safety incidents (and near misses). This is discussed in detail in chapter 24.

INVESTIGATE
EVALUATE

How these activities are done is as important as doing them. A supervisor who treats these things as a "necessary evil," appears disinterested, or who fails to involve front-line employees can under-mine the entire safety effort. On the other hand, a supervisor who performs these activities well demonstrates leadership and dedica-tion, creates an environment in which employees are committed to safety, and generally builds a more effective work team. Doing these activities well means having meaningful content *and* doing the activ-ity with appropriate use of safety leadership skills.

By clarifying expectations of supervisors, helping them learn to do these activities effectively, and holding them accountable for these activities, managers can have a major impact on safety, as well as on overall organizational performance.

ENGAGEMENT FOR FRONT-LINE WORKERS

Many organizations have adopted behavior-based safety as an approach to increased employee engagement. As with many successful business tools, initial popularity led to a fad that created a great deal of confusion. The behavior-based safety label came to be applied to a number of methods with a wide variation in results. One method that has been extensively studied, and which can be called comprehensive behavior-based safety, provides a good example of how to create effective employee engagement.

A comprehensive behavior-based safety process is a system in which front-line workers identify the most important at-risk behaviors (behaviors that are indicative of high exposure to injury).[1] Workers are trained to gather data on the prevalence of those behaviors, usually through a peer-to-peer observation process conducted while preserving the anonymity of the observed workers. As workers perform these observations they do two things. First, when they observe the critical behaviors performed safely they provide feedback to the observed worker, reinforcing the safe behavior. Second, when they observe a behavior performed at risk they discuss with the observed worker why that is occurring. The observation is documented so that data is generated on which behaviors are most often performed at-risk and why, and the data are used by a combination of front-line workers and managers to address the underlying reasons for at-risk behavior. This entire process is managed by a team of workers together with a management sponsor, and includes active communication to everyone regarding what is being found and what barriers to safe behavior are being addressed.

Comparing this approach to the criteria described above for effective employee participation, it is clear why a comprehensive and well-implemented behavior-based safety process is extremely effective approach to achieving engagement. History shows that comprehensive, well-implemented behavior-based safety processes contribute to significant injury reduction over many years, improve hazard

[1] For more information, see *The Behavior-Based Safety Process, Second Ed.*, by Thomas R. Krause (Hoboken: Wiley, 1997.)

recognition and communications, and identify and help resolve previously unrecognized barriers to safety. Whether behavior-based safety or some other approach is used, an organization harnessing the power of broad employee engagement is well positioned for continuous improvement in safety.

SUSTAINING ENGAGEMENT

For managers, the most important lesson is that engagement does not occur in a vacuum. Individuals usually have long histories with each other, with their manager, and with the organization as a whole. At the front-line level, a series of supervisors may have come and gone, and each one probably focused on one area and neglected others. Sustaining engagement will depend on creating a culture that supports active participation and open communication. We discuss culture further in chapters 26 and 27.

LEARNING FROM EXPERIENCE

As in other areas of performance, in safety it is important to learn from experiences, both good and bad. One way to do this is by understanding how to use safety data to increase your understanding and focus your efforts. Another way is by using incidents and near misses as opportunities to understand the strengths and weaknesses of your safety efforts.

This section discusses how best to use data and incident investigation.

CHAPTER TWENTY-THREE

USING SAFETY DATA:
Optimizing the Value

*Information is the oil of the 21st century,
and analytics is the combustion engine.*
—Peter Sondergaard, senior vice president Gartner

Over the last several years, there has been a tremendous growth both in the sheer amount of data collected (by some estimates growing by 30-40% per year) and in the tools available to analyze and draw insight from this information. For decision makers, it can be difficult to cut through the jargon to find what is most effective, particularly as it relates to safety. As a manager, you need not be a data expert to lead safety. But you do need to know how to navigate information effectively. This chapter describes the pitfalls and principles of data use in safety.

CREATING INSIGHT, NOT NOISE

Elsewhere in this book we have discussed safety metrics and the importance of defining and implementing meaningful leading and lagging metrics. When those data are available, what should we be doing with them? Leveraging safety data is an unexploited opportunity in many organizations, while misusing data leads others down the wrong path. In using safety data, it is helpful to apply the following principles:

Look at trends, not single data points

Many things influence what we measure in safety, and metrics tend to show some amount of fluctuation simply due to normal variation in the underlying influences. As a result it is a mistake to overreact to a single data point, whether good or bad.

Trends in data are more meaningful than single data points. To be able to assess trends, data must be normalized and reported in formats that make trends visible. The typical report showing the most recent period versus plan, or versus the corresponding period in the prior year, fails to illuminate trends. Request data in the format of run charts over time (see Figure 23-1)—not just restarting each year but spanning longer periods (e.g., two or three years) to fully show trends. This allows you to recognize when performance is plateaued and when it is truly changing.

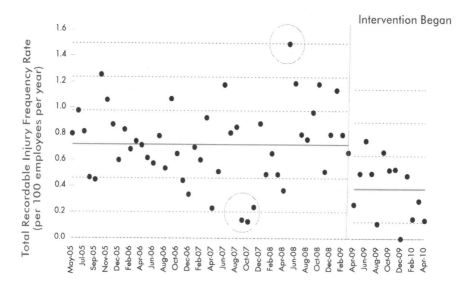

Figure 23-1. Sample control chart.

Look beyond the high-level aggregation

In most organizations data is rolled up so that senior leaders are looking only at the aggregation of results from many individual departments and units. While the rolled-up data does provide information on overall performance, it masks important information about what is happening within the organization. It is entirely possible for the total organization to show an overall small level of improvement while more than half of the operating units are experiencing declining performance.

Senior executives do not want to be buried under massive amounts of detail, but neither should they allow themselves to be fooled by aggregation. One approach to addressing this dilemma is to get data on the top 10% and bottom 10% of facilities (or departments, or whatever unit is applicable to the scope of your responsibility). When the top and bottom performers are defined in terms of the performance trend (so that individual period anomalies are eliminated), this enables you to give reinforcement to top performers and ask appropriate questions of bottom performers.

The level of detail that you need to focus on varies depending on your role. It is impractical and inadvisable for senior executives to be looking at an exhaustive breakdown of data from every workgroup, but it is equally inappropriate for a site manager to look only at his site level or overall company data. A general rule to follow is that managers at each level need to look at enough data to understand the performance of the organizations two levels below them, so they can ask appropriate questions and supply appropriate positive reinforcement and guidance to their direct reports. An example of what information might be reported at various organizational levels is included at the end of this chapter.

Consider statistical significance

The annual injury frequency rate is the most commonly used safety metric. The most common form of this rate reflects the number of injuries per 200,000 hours (or sometimes per one million hours) worked. Managers often watch this rate carefully and react to small changes. However injury rate is often the source of misinterpretation by managers. When a period of time passes with no injuries, most people conclude that safety performance has been good; conversely, when several injuries occur within a short period, the typical assumption is that safety performance has deteriorated.

It is a fundamental fact that a stable safety system will produce a variable number of injury events. That is, due to the large number of factors influencing whether an injury occurs, the number of injuries is unlikely to be identical from month to month even when there is no change at all in hazards, controls, or production. To understand the significance of injury rate changes, we must make statistical comparison of these outcomes with the predicted random outcome for the operation in question. Simply reacting to changes without understanding their statistical significance leads to misinterpretation and can produce false feedback to the operations in question.

For example, consider a workgroup of 100 employees. It is easy for their injury rate to change from 2.0 over a 12-month period to 4.0 for the most recent quarter with no real change in the safety system. The prior 12-month period reflects two injuries, and the most recent quarter reflects one injury. Given the workgroup size, the quarterly increase to 4.0 is not significant (special cause variation), and in fact must occur at some point during the year when the annual rate is 2.0. Unfortunately in the field of safety, many reward systems and performance appraisals are based on numerical goals and measures that are untested for statistical significance. For the supervisors of this hypothetical workgroup, this could well mean receiving a bad performance rating that is undeserved.

The important point is to be sure to understand the statistical significance of variations that occur in safety metrics before you act on them.

Use data to drive actions

In many organizations safety metrics are distributed on a monthly basis to managers who do not really know what to do with the information. The most obvious reaction is to use the data to reward high performers and/or to refer to the data in communications. While there is nothing wrong with either of those uses, if that is the only thing you do with the data, you are missing some important opportunities.

Safety metrics allow you to target and focus safety improvement efforts. Good safety data use goes beyond just reporting the number of events (whether injuries in lagging data or activities in leading data). It provides information on which exposures in the workplace are causing injuries, and which may have an increasing exposure profile even before injuries occur. A key weakness of many safety efforts is that activities such as monthly safety meetings are done "out of habit" with no real consideration of whether the exposures they impact are really important to the location. Effective use of data allows you to fine-tune the safety programs and assure they address the most important exposures.

The most effective mechanism you have for assuring that data are used effectively is to ask questions. In reviewing operations, you have insight into the most important exposures, ask how those are being addressed. In doing facility tours, ask workers at all levels about those specific exposures. Show both your awareness of the issues and your concern, and you will also learn how well the safety effort is working. When you use data well, you reinforce the organization's value for safety in a concrete and impactful way.

Understand influences and confounding factors

Always approach data as the start of the discussion. Any time the metrics show improvement or decline, ask why. Both leading and lagging indicator data can be misleading if you don't consider what factors might be influencing them.

For example, a location may be showing a trend of improving injury rate well in excess of the overall organizations' performance. The savvy leader seeks to understand what is happening at the location to produce that result. It could be that this location is using a different safety improvement initiative that is bearing fruit—a very important thing to know! But there can also be other explanations. It's possible that the location has recently reduced production in response to lower demand. Perhaps they have outsourced some of the higher-hazard work to contractors. Maybe they implemented an incentive program that inadvertently discourages workers from reporting injuries. Regardless, the effective leader will not be content with seeing apparent improvement and offering congratulations; she will be sure to inquire into the cause—and to assure that the data reflect true improvement in reducing exposure.

Conversely, when a location shows a trend of deteriorating performance, the key question again is why. It may be that less support is being given to safety in the face of production pressure, but it may be that a new process has increased the exposure profile. Again, the trend may reflect external factors, such as weather. Perhaps a major expansion has introduced a large number of new, inexperienced workers. To determine whether management is dropping the ball or is trying hard in the face of exceptional challenges it's critical to understand what is behind the data.

Don't lose the forest for the trees

Even after you understand how to think about safety data, you still need to decide what data is appropriate for you to review. It is not uncommon for managers to be presented with reams of safety data at a management meeting because the well-intentioned safety staff doesn't know what to present and managers don't know how to guide them. As a result we see every variable that is captured on an incident-investigation form charted, tabled, and spread sheeted in glorious detail for all to see. This data overload prevents managers from having meaningful discussions. Establish the expectation with your staff that the data presented answers the questions: What is the data telling us, and what do you recommend we do about it?

Understanding how to interpret and summarize data may not be a skill possessed by safety staff. In that case, managers should provide mentoring. Encourage the presentation of interpreted data even if you disagree with the conclusions. The data analyst won't get it right every time: None of us do. Be patient. If staff make a mistake and leave the meeting feeling belittled and unsponsored it will be hard to get them to continue to work on developing this skill.

The process of interpreting the data will do several things. Two of the most important are instilling a scientific approach to inquiry and a focus on why (causation) versus simply describing what happened. For example, it is not unusual for safety data to show that more accidents happen on the day shift. However, since most organizations have more people working on day shift this shouldn't be surprising. The real question is whether the frequency normalized for hours worked is statistically significantly higher or lower than expected. This would be meaningful. Good interpretation also eliminates the creation of graphs and tables just because we have the data, and instead helps to focus discussion and action on where exposure reduction is needed. For example, many organizations' data shows that hand injuries represent a large proportion of all injuries. We know that the majority of work is done with our hands, so this outcome isn't unexpected. But what would be truly helpful to understand is the configuration of exposures that are contributing to these injuries. This allows implementation of a focused approach to deal with a specific type of exposure (e.g., people placing their hands in pinch points) rather than only being able to generically tell people to protect their hands.

Review safety metrics along with other operating metrics

Wherever possible, include consideration of safety metrics along with the review of other operating metrics. This reinforces the idea that safety is one of the key business parameters and also provides a more complete picture of how well different parts of the organization are performing.

Report appropriate data for each level of the organization

Many organizations struggle to find a happy medium for reporting safety data. They are unsure of what data to report and end up either reporting inadequate data or too much detail. The example that follows is based on the principle of giving each level of the organization the information that it needs to know, with the level of detail increasing as the organizational level gets closer to the working interface.

Individuals at any level should have the option of digging into a greater level of detail to answer specific questions. What's important is not allowing them to become "buried" in routine data packages with so much detail that the important messages of the data are lost.

REPORTING

Examples of the types of safety data to report by organizational level:

Executive leadership

- Statistical control charts of injury trends organization wide.
- Variation of safety performance across business units and a focus on statistically significant variation.
- Statistical control charts of serious injury and fatality potential rates by business unit.
- The status of high-profile safety initiatives and activities (e.g., focused on catastrophic event prevention, culture change or safety leadership development or significant changes to the safety and health management system).
- Organization level opportunities for improvement that come from the interpretation of the data and that require their knowledge and support.

Business unit leadership

- Statistical control charts of injury trends for the business unit.
- Variation of safety performance across locations within the business unit with a focus on statistically significant variation.
- Statistical control charts of serious injury and fatality potential rates by location.
- The status of high-profile safety initiatives and activities.
- Business unit level opportunities that come from the interpretation of the data.

Location level leadership

- Statistical control charts of injury trends for the location.
- Variation of safety performance across departments with a focus on statistically significant variation
- Statistical control charts of serious injury and fatality potential rates
- Location level opportunities for improvement that come from the interpretation of the data
- The status of high-profile safety initiative and activities

Front-line employees

- Reporting of raw numbers of injury events versus prior periods.
- The status of high-profile safety initiatives and activities.
- Location level opportunities for improvement that come from the interpretation of the data.

DATA-DRIVEN SAFETY

Effective use of a good set of safety metrics is key to an effective, continuously improving safety effort. Managers must do more than review and acknowledge safety data reports; you must seek to understand the real meaning of the data and prompt effective data-based action within your organization.

CHAPTER TWENTY-FOUR
INCIDENT HANDLING

There is nothing quite like a crisis to test your leadership. It will make or break you as a leader.
—BILL GEORGE, FORMER CEO MEDTRONIC

Whether it is in the midst of a steady stream of low-potential injuries, a rash of near misses, or a single serious injury that seems to come out of the blue, handling an incident presents a manager with one of the toughest challenges he or she will ever face. What do you say? What do you do—and in what order? This chapter outlines the principles and practices essential to effective incident handling.

THE IMPORTANCE OF RESPONSE

When a safety incident occurs how does your organization respond? Is the primary focus on determining the reporting requirement for the event? Is the focus on handling the outcomes—that is, caring for injured individuals, containing damage, etc.? Or is the focus on capturing information and completing an investigation? All three of these elements are important parts of the overall incident handling system. The system's starting point is the identification and reporting of an incident. The endpoint is where the action items identified from the incident investigation have been completed and it has been verified that those actions are having the desired impact and are sustainable.

These three elements must be integrated as well as individually effective. The integrity of any one of the elements is influenced by that of the others. There are several important attributes that an incident handling system. In an effective system:

1. Employees leave the experience feeling that management recognizes something important and undesired has happened to the employee and that management truly cares about the employee's safety and well-being.
2. Reporting is unencumbered by systems or cultural barriers.
3. Investigation occurs to the level appropriate given the incident's potential.
4. Immediate and root causes are clearly identified.
5. Action items are developed that result in documented, sustained change.

HOW NOT TO HANDLE AN INCIDENT

An employee tells his supervisor that he has strained his back. "Do you want to file a report?" asks the supervisor, "Because if you do it means a lot of paperwork, a drug test, and lots of questions being asked of you about how you could have avoided this accident. Do you think that something you did at home could have caused this strain?" The employee presses the issue and elects to report the strain. The supervisor takes down the information about how the strain happened and sends out a flash report to site management. Shortly afterward, someone from management responds, "You don't think the case will end up being a recordable injury, do you?"

This scenario provides a useful insight into a dysfunctional incident-handling system. While the report was filed as required, there were two not-so-subtle indicators of how this organization's managers and supervisors really think about and respond to incidents:

*   The supervisor's reaction that reporting would be a lot of work tells the employee that the organizations' value for safety, the likelihood of accurate reporting, and the probability of getting to all the root causes are all fairly low.
*   Management's question about reporting status says that the real concern is doing what it takes to avoid the injury

becoming recordable (i.e., looking bad) rather than understanding root causes and working to correct them.

Both the employee and the supervisor receive a clear message that reporting an incident is not valued. In this organization, it's more important to avoid burdening the supervisor or the organization itself with the work of an incident than it is to support the employee.

In these situations, the absence of a demonstration of true concern for the employee is glaring. And when you point this out, many leaders will become understandably defensive. "Of course we make sure the employee is taken care of first," they will tell you. That may well have been their intention. However, when you talk to the employee involved, he will say that he remembers everything but the feeling that leadership really cared about him.

There are many reasons that an incident handling system can end up dysfunctional. Let's consider each of the three parts of the system.

Incident reporting

Incident reporting is the mechanism by which an employee brings attention to one of three types of safety issue: an injury, a malfunction or damage to equipment, or a near miss or close call. For most organizations this mechanism calls for the employee to report the situation to her immediate supervisor. Incident reporting includes several basic elements.

Assessing the situation

The first task for the supervisor is to determine the seriousness of the event. The supervisor needs to collect as much information as possible about what happened. Fact finding supports incident investigation and it helps determine reportability (how the injury will be classified). Fact finding is secondary to taking care of affected individuals.

The interaction between employee and supervisor here sets the tone for the rest of the incident handling system. In this rare and small window, the employee sees with stark clarity the extent of management's seriousness about safety and the depth of her supervisor's concern for her. If the supervisor conveys that his primary interest is in finding a way to blame the employee, credibility will be damaged and the chances of collaborative problem solving will be undermined.

There are two aspects to how the supervisor's response sets the tone. First, does the supervisor focus on information gathering with apparent priority over dealing with an injured employee and/or a physical hazard? Second, does the supervisor keep an open mind about what happened or jump to the conclusion that the worker must be at fault?

Notification

Most organizations have a notification system (flash reporting) that kicks in depending on the severity of the incident. These systems are beneficial in letting senior leadership know that an incident has happened and that the on-site leader is handling the situation. However these systems can become disruptive when they prompt senior leaders to jump into the middle of the situation, firing off emails or calls to ask questions or challenging decisions or raising questions about whether the incident will be recordable. While it is understandable that senior leaders want people to know they have gotten the report and are concerned, it would be better to allow the incident response to run its course.

After the incident has been resolved, if the leader believes that there is an improvement opportunity, then initiating a lessons learned discussion is in order. The worst time to be doing lessons learned is in the middle of an incident. This tends to be seen as second guessing local management and results in managers being less willing to take initiative and make decisions in the future.

Incident response

Incident response is the procedure management follows when there has been an injury, chemical release, fire, explosion, or major equipment damage. This part of the incident handling system clarifies how to handle each type of incident and who has what responsibilities.

Obviously, if there has been an injury the most critical focus is making sure the employee's injury and needs are taken care of. Additionally, it is important that the scene where the incident happened not be compromised so fact finding can happen.

For many organizations incident response procedures fail to consider the off-shift or off-site scenario where there are few (or even no) managers or supervisors on site who can provide support. Planning for incident response should consider minimal staffing situations, such as where there is one supervisor on night shift who is responsible for "everything."

What is this person's primary priority when the incident occurs? Is it to make sure the employee's needs are addressed? To control the scene? To assure there is adequate clean up if there is a spill or release? To assure that employees are in compliance with the blood-borne pathogens policy? To do what is necessary to get production restarted? To assure the injured employee is drug tested? The plan for incident response should consider how to address all of these issues while demonstrating care and concern for the employee.

Incident investigation and closure

The final element of the incident handling system is the investigation. While the "what" information has been collected at the reporting stage, the formal investigation process is used to get to the "why." The purpose of the investigation is four fold:

- Identify immediate causal factors (unsafe condition or at-risk behavior).
- Identify root causal factors (additional unsafe conditions, at-risk behavior, systems or cultural factors).
- Develop a set of action items that will address the immediate and/or root causal factors.
- Identify a mechanism for assuring the action items are having the desired impact and that the change is sustainable.

There will always be at least one immediate cause and most often one or more root cause factors.

THE CHALLENGES OF INCIDENT INVESTIGATION

While the common problems with incident reporting and incident response are fairly straightforward, the problems that surface in incident investigation are more complex and fall into several broad categories:

Completing an investigation in 24 or 48 hours

An interesting and baffling part of many incident handling systems is the requirement that the investigation be completed in 24 hours. This requirement may have begun due to the importance of collecting as much information as possible within a 24-hour window because memories can change and the physical conditions at the location can be changed. Another reason this rule might exist is belief that it demonstrates management's seriousness about safety. However we need to consider the unintended consequences for setting up a system that suggests that a high quality investigation is desired, but limits the organization to a 24-hour period to complete it.

The limitations of this approach can be seen in the following example: An employee reports being sprayed in the eye when a line she was breaking released a chemical. The employee reports that she was not wearing goggles or a face shield, because when she went to the storeroom to get a replacement for the scratched and oil-smeared ones in the crew box, the storeroom said that they didn't have any in stock. The employee said she didn't see the situation as a big risk since she was wearing safety glasses with side shields.

The supervisor responsible for doing the incident investigation goes to the storeroom supervisor to talk about the inventory of face shields and safety goggles. The storeroom supervisor says there was a change in the inventory policy, which required keeping minimal inventory levels and relying on just-in-time delivery. The storeroom looked at typical usage per week for each item and kept a standing order for that amount. The storeroom supervisor said that this policy came from the accounting department.

Off to the accounting department the supervisor goes to discuss safety supply inventory. The accounting manager listens to the supervisor's concern but says that the inventory policy came from corporate. Reducing inventory was a way to help control cash flow. To get relief from the requirement requires site manager approval.

In addition to the storeroom issue the supervisor must look into why equipment in the crew box is being left in such poor condition and consider how to fix that system. Finally, the supervisor must consider the cultural issue where an employee runs into barriers to safely completing a job and does not raise the concern with the supervisor.

Given the complexity of even this simple example, completing the investigation in 24 hours, including development of quality action items and methods for assuring that the action items have been effective, seems unrealistic.

The simple example also illustrates several points at which the quality of incident investigation can break down:

- People may not have the skills to do the type of investigation described.
- People may not have the time to conduct this thorough of an incident investigation.
- The people who lead incident investigations may require help to put together an effective set of action items and an approach to determine if the action items are effective and lead to sustained change.

Failing to differentiate based on potential

It is not practical or necessary to do an in-depth incident review in every case, but it is important to do so when there was the potential for serious outcomes (even if those serious outcomes were averted). A good incident handling system assures that the appropriate level of review is given to every incident by following several important principles:

1. The expectation is set that all incidents are to be reported. Clarify that just because something gets reported doesn't mean that there will be a root cause investigation.
2. A mechanism is created to evaluate whether the incident had serious injury and fatality potential.
3. For low-potential incidents two investigation mechanisms are established. First an abbreviated investigation occurs to assure there are no immediate items that need to be addressed to prevent recurrence. Second collect the data and on a routine basis look for a high number of low-potential incidents that have similar immediate causes. Conduct a deeper investigation on this pattern.
4. For high-potential incidents, investigate each one but apply more rigor to the investigation and development of the action plan. If another high-potential incident happens, after a preliminary investigation has occurred, determine if any other incident or incidents that involved the same root causal factors have happened. Review the status of the action plan and see if it is adequate or if it was fully implemented. It is likely that there is great knowledge to be gleaned by looking longitudinally at the incidents.

Narrow focus

In most organizations each incident investigation is conducted, reviewed, and communicated as an isolated event. When that happens, the opportunity is missed to conduct longitudinal analysis — looking across multiple incidents and incident investigations to identify common themes and common factors. Failing to look longitudinally can result in addressing one manifestation of an underlying issue without addressing the underlying issue itself. In the example used earlier in this chapter, the investigation identified a corporate policy that had gotten in the way of safety. However if we looked at a group of investigations and saw several examples of various corporate policies emanating from different corporate departments that each in its own way impeded safety, we might recognize a need to systematically address policy setting. That latter conclusion would be much less likely to emerge from a single instance.

Negative consequences tied to incident reporting

While it may seem counterintuitive to suggest that in the future we want more rather than fewer incidents reported, however that should be the vision for the system. With more reporting comes the opportunity to detect changes in exposure and the ability to look at groupings of common incidents. In combination with observation and auditing systems that look at behavior, conditions, and the effectiveness of systems this gives the organization the information needed to excel in safety.

The biggest challenge to getting thorough reporting is the connection of negative consequences to the behavior of reporting an incident. Negative consequences can include: drug testing; completion of long, complicated forms even for the lowest of potential of incidents; asking the employee to document what they could have done to prevent the incident; point systems where reporting results in points and accumulation of points leads to inclusion in a system for "problem" employees; losing an incentive or bonus; discipline (when incident investigation is one of the few places where discipline is actually handed out for safety), etc.

To get complete reporting an organization should identify the negative consequences tied to incident reporting and remove as many as you can. For example, if you believe that you have a drug-abuse problem in the workplace that is causing accidents, implement a more rigorous random drug-testing system to deal with the problem before an accident happens. If you are using incentives, stop tying incentives to injury rates and move to a more upstream and proactive measure. In some organizations the use of anonymous near miss reporting is used to encourage complete reporting, but this approach makes it very difficult to get to root causes and so is far less effective than eliminating the deterrents to reporting.

Ineffective communications

A friend and colleague once shared a story that happened to him. After he had made a presentation to the CEO, the CEO asked him to stay behind for a moment as the other people in the room filed out. The CEO told the individual how well he had handled the meeting and that it was obvious he was well prepared. The CEO then gave him one piece of advice: "Tell me what I need to know, not everything you know."

This advice holds true for communicating about incident investigations. The incident investigation for a serious incident is likely to be complex and involve extensive information, from interviews to data analyses. It is easy for people to get lost in the minutiae and lose sight of the forest for the trees if the detail is presented. What is important in communicating the results is to focus on the big picture about the root causes and how to address them. This places attention where it belongs—on how to prevent recurrence of this and similar incidents.

BETTER INVESTIGATIONS

Incident handling involves reporting, response, and investigation, and these should occur in an integrated and coordinated way that reinforces the organization's desire to take care of employees and continuously improve safety by reducing exposure. Creating an incident-handling system that achieves those objectives requires pre-planning and the avoidance of pitfalls.

CHAPTER TWENTY-FIVE

THE ROLE OF COGNITIVE BIAS IN SAFETY DECISIONS

Bad decisions made with good intentions,
are still bad decisions.
—JIM COLLINS, AUTHOR GOOD TO GREAT

Many safety-related decisions require that managers make accurate judgments about future likelihoods. After an undesirable outcome, it often seems clear what should have been decided. When we look carefully at what we knew before the event, we often see that we had all the information we needed to make a safety-supporting decision, but we didn't pay attention to it. Why not? A rich scientific literature in cognitive psychology helps explain this seemingly irrational phenomenon: human beings tend to make inaccurate judgments about future probabilities in predictable ways. These tendencies toward faulty judgments are called cognitive biases, and they can lead to serious safety problems.

HIDDEN TRAPS IN DECISION MAKING

In an otherwise complex world, cognitive biases allow us to establish shortcuts that simplify decision making, make our world more predictable, and absorb new information consistently with what we already know. Cognitive biases are automatic and unconscious. They shape how human beings select and process information.

Leaders can make most decisions without a purposeful consideration of cognitive bias. Cognitive bias can be disastrous, however, at critical decision points. Therefore, it is important to appreciate the role cognitive bias can play. Cognitive bias can cause leaders to underestimate exposure risk and overestimate the capability of systems to mitigate hazards. While any single decision may be insignificant by itself, a series of small, incorrect decisions may create a path to disaster.

The purpose of this chapter is to acquaint you with cognitive bias and help you devise strategies for avoiding the errors it can create.

TRAGEDY ON MOUNT EVEREST

On May 10, 1996, five mountain climbers perished in an attempt to reach the summit of Mount Everest. Two were the world-renowned mountaineers Rob Hall and Scott Fischer, both skilled team leaders with extensive experience climbing at high altitudes. Hall was the leader of the Adventure Consultants expedition and had successfully guided almost 40 climbers to the summit over the previous six years. Fischer, leader of the Mountain Madness expedition, had reached the Everest summit only once, but he had a reputation as a skilled high-altitude climber. Climbing Everest has always been challenging and potentially dangerous: Between 1922 and 1996 more than 160 people had died attempting to reach the summit.

No single reason explains the 1996 tragedy; instead, a complex amalgam of causes, including deficient team functioning and flawed decision making, contributed to the outcome. The story provides an opportunity to study the way leaders shape behavior while balancing competing pressures within their teams or organizations. It shows how their words and actions influence perceptions and beliefs that can lead to hazardous behaviors. This case, described in California Management Review,[1] provides a particularly good explication of cognitive bias because it occurred within a complex system encompassing multiple interactions, much like the ones facing safety leaders.

[1] Michael A. Roberto, "Lessons from Everest: The Interaction of Cognitive Bias, Psychological Safety, and System Complexity," *California Management Review*, 45 (Fall 2002): pp. 136-158.

As background, the situation that prevailed prior to the Mount Everest tragedy can be characterized as follows:

- High-level mountain climbing was acknowledged as a challenging and potentially dangerous sport. Climbing Mount Everest was known to be particularly dangerous.
- The expedition leaders, Rob Hall and Scott Fischer, were highly skilled experts. They had exceptional reputations as guides and had a history of successful ascents at high altitudes.
- The clients (the participants in the climb) had invested significant resources (as much as $70,000 each) and expected to reach the summit of Everest.
- The participants had prepared for the physical rigors of the climb and were confident in their abilities.
- Agreed-upon guidelines shared by the Adventure Consultants and Mountain Madness expeditions helped to manage risk—e.g., the "two-o'clock rule" stated: "If you're not at the summit by 2:00 p.m. at the latest, you must turn around."
- There had been a recent history of favorable climbing weather.

Of the dozens of climbers ascending the summit that day, only six reached the top of Everest by 2:00 p.m. Around that time, four of the remaining climbers abandoned their bid for the summit in order to begin their descent. Hall and Fischer, however, continued toward the summit with 15 others. Some of these climbers arrived as late as 4:00 p.m. When unexpected bad weather developed, poor visibility overcame the climbers, resulting in five fatalities between the two expeditions.

Cognitive bias played a significant role in the fatal decisions. Three types of bias were particularly noteworthy:

- OVERCONFIDENCE BIAS—A tendency to overestimate the accuracy of your predictions, despite evidence to the contrary. Both the guides and their clients exhibited this bias: They felt confident about their success even though the data on successful ascents of Mount Everest did not justify it.

- SUNK COST BIAS—A tendency to make choices that support past decisions and escalate your commitment to a course of action in which you have invested, even when data indicate you may be on a losing course. After investing so much in the climb, the guides and clients did not follow the two o'clock rule to which they had previously agreed.

- RECENCY BIAS—A tendency to pay more attention to data that are recent and easy to recall. The recent history of very favorable climbing weather overshadowed the known probability of violent storms.

COGNITIVE BIAS IN WORKPLACE SAFETY

Safety leaders make decisions under many different pressures while managing the risks inherent in the workplace and seeking to satisfy a variety of constituencies. These pressures often do not explain mistaken decisions that in hindsight were preventable. For example, what causes a leader to keep a poor performing supervisor who fails to improve despite repeated coaching or another to postpone equipment repair that would reduce exposure?

Cognitive bias can cause leaders to underestimate exposure risk and overestimate the capability of systems to mitigate hazards. While any single decision may be insignificant by itself, a series of small decisions can lead to a catastrophic outcome.

Some of the biases that affect safety decisions include:

Anchoring

Anchoring describes the tendency to give disproportionate weight to the first information received or to a specific piece of information over all others, allowing the initial or preferred information to "anchor" subsequent judgments.

When faced with an incident or when discussing what to do about a safety problem, how often does the first idea for which there is some evidence capture the group's attention and come to dominate subsequent thought, discussion, and action to the exclusion of other causes, such as cultural and systems issues?

Attribution Bias

Attribution error biases operate through the tendency to understand one's own success in terms of personal powers and abilities while seeing one's failings as the result of bad luck or external, situational causes. Conversely, we also suffer from the tendency to explain others' failings in terms of dispositional factors (i.e., internal factors such as personality or an inadequate sense of responsibility). For example, if someone else—particularly someone you do not like—gets in a car accident, it's probably because he is such a bad driver. If you get into a car accident, it's because the roads were slippery. This bias is self-serving because it excuses our own failings while blaming others for theirs. It leads immediately to (spoken or unspoken) blame as the first response to a problem.

At the group level, the group attribution error acts in the same way to protect my group identifications from members of other groups—whether defined by race, gender, belief system, or in other ways. This phenomenon creates the in-group bias (below).

In-group bias

This is the tendency to give preferential treatment to members of one's own group. This bias strengthens subculture alignment at the expense of alignment with the larger culture. For example, it may pit supervisors against line employees or line employees against management. In an unhealthy culture, in-group bias can defeat the successful investigation of incidents when those involved act to protect group members.

Recency (or availability/non availability) bias

Recency is the tendency to rely on those data that are most readily available (e.g., most noticeable or recent) and therefore easiest to remember, while neglecting less readily available data. In the Everest case recent good weather helped people decide they could overlook the "two-o'clock rule" although that rule was based on long experience of the weather on the mountain. Availability bias and anchoring are the most frequent biases at work in hectic, high-pressure situations such as a project environment.

Sunk cost bias

Sunk cost bias is the tendency to make choices that support past decisions and escalate our commitment to a course of action in which we have invested time, energy, reputation, or money—even when data indicate this course of action may be a mistake. This bias—clear in the Everest case—manifests itself as a lack of flexibility (i.e., a difficulty recognizing when to change course). For example, a leader may not comprehend that the safety data are flashing a warning signal about the course of action to which she previously committed.

Status quo bias

Status quo bias is the tendency to filter information so as to favor the current situation. Employees at every level may be subject to this bias when considering whether to support organizational and cultural change. This preconception is another bias that often underlies the objection, "We don't have a safety problem here."

Overconfidence bias and optimism bias

Leaders and managers alike tend to overestimate the accuracy of our predictions, perceptions, and judgments as well as the strength of our abilities, even in the presence of evidence to the contrary. Similarly, we tend to be overly optimistic about the success of a course of action to which we have committed. In safety, these biases may show up as an inability to see the warning signs that an intervention is not working. Perhaps, for example, the leader assumes that because he has deployed the intervention, the organization is following it, and he fails to notice the telltale signs that it is not. These biases can also color how we estimate an intervention's likelihood of success.

Rosy retrospection

This is the tendency to look back and remember the "good ol' days." We recall our successes with a procedure or system more readily than we recall our failures. This predisposition distorts our judgment when we contemplate giving up a familiar procedure in favor of a new one. It may even blind us to the failure of the familiar procedure to produce the outcomes we ascribe to it. It is part of what motivates resistance to change.

PUTTING YOUR COGNITIVE BIAS KNOWLEDGE TO WORK

How can a manager put this knowledge to work? During important decisions, successful decision makers use their working knowledge of cognitive bias to self-monitor and to enlist others in the effort to monitor for cognitive bias. For the manager and safety leader whose choices affect the success with which exposure to hazards is controlled, this exercise can be critically important.

Frame the issue

- First, consider the problem on your own, then gather input from others.
- Don't be stampeded. Resist unreasonable pressures to make immediate decisions. Cultivate the ability to approach emergencies and other high-pressure situations with a degree of mental calmness.
- Consider how the problem has been framed by yourself or others. What history does it bring? What assumptions? How much momentum?
- Seek to widen your frame of reference and look at the problem with fresh eyes.
- Ask others how they are inclined to frame the issue.

Select the data

- Consider the prototypes the situation invokes, and look for other mental models that might be important to consider, especially models whose neglect represents a serious error.
- Discuss with others the data they would consider, seek data from a variety of sources, and intentionally attend to data that discount your theory.
- Consider whether you are anchored in the wrong data.
- Ask yourself what forms the basis of your assessment. Do you have valid and applicable data, or are you acting on recency or status quo bias?

Judge available options

- Ask about alternative choices, interpretations, and decisions, and define competing options clearly. The status quo is never your only option and your choices are rarely binary (i.e., to act or not act). In important decisions, always generate a short list of alternatives.
- For all decisions with history, verify that you are not giving undue consideration to sunk costs.

- Identify a credible team member or other person to play your devil's advocate.
- Ask yourself what your emotions are telling you to do and whether their guidance is appropriate.

Learning from your mistakes

- Study the research on cognitive bias and encourage other safety leaders to do the same.
- Seek help from colleagues to dissect erroneous decisions to uncover the cognitive errors involved, their triggers, and what might have prevented the errors.

Most important, the successful manager understands that the culture influences the extent to which errors of cognitive bias are allowed to flourish. A culture in which open communication is encouraged and mistakes are openly shared and dissected is the best protection against the potentially detrimental effects of cognitive bias.

MAKING BETTER DECISIONS

Knowledge of cognitive bias enables managers to question their own thinking and to isolate biases that increase hazards. In addition to becoming acquainted with the literature on cognitive bias, safety leaders can improve their decision making by putting this knowledge to use when weighing important issues. Managers who monitor themselves for the effect of biases in their thinking, and who enlist others in the effort to check for bias, can improve the quality of safety decisions and the outcomes they produce. Understanding cognitive bias won't change every decision a manager makes, but knowledge of its effects can inform the decision-making process. Most importantly, this knowledge provides a strong incentive for managers to engage in open communication, to share and dissect mistakes openly, and to foster a culture that strongly favors effective safety functioning.

SAFETY CULTURE

Every workplace has a discernible way that things are done. How we make decisions and approach tasks, apply concepts and execute directives are all strongly influenced by our culture—the shared values and beliefs of the organization. For managers, it is not enough to simply know what to do in safety, they must also understand the context in which things are being done.

This section provides an overview of culture as it pertains to safety.

CHAPTER TWENTY-SIX

UNDERSTANDING AND CHANGING CULTURE

When strategy conflicts with culture,
strategy doesn't stand a chance.
—ANONYMOUS

Keeping employees safe requires reliable systems that are operating well and used consistently across the organization. Employees must also work with each other, across departments, between shifts, even when their immediate interests may be in conflict. In an ideal world, managers and supervisors enable this collaboration by creating a positive safety climate and culture. Realistically, issues such as low trust, poor communication, and friction between workgroups or levels are common. We see the effects of culture all the time: how (or whether) people engage the work, go "above and beyond" stated duties, speak up about exposures, and so on. What role does culture and climate really play in safety, and what can managers do to create safety as a driving value?

CULTURE, CLIMATE, AND SAFETY

When managers hear the terms *culture* and *climate*, these terms often sound too vague to be helpful. In this book we mean something specific and measurable by these terms. Culture and climate are related but distinct concepts:

- ORGANIZATIONAL CULTURE—The shared, often unconscious values, attitudes, standards, and assumptions that govern behavior, especially in situations that lack clearly defined rules and procedures. Organizational culture is the driving values of the organization—"the way things are done around here." Culture is manifested in concrete and quantifiable organizational characteristics that lend themselves to measurement and intervention.

- SAFETY CLIMATE—The prevailing, usually consciously held perception of leadership's priority for a particular area of functioning (safety in this case) at a particular time. It reveals to workers with immediacy and urgency how leaders want them to respond in the face of conflicting priorities.

Organizational culture is deeply embedded and long term; it takes longer to change and it drives organizational performance across many areas of functioning. Safety climate, on the other hand, changes faster and more immediately, and a climate change, when sustained, reshapes culture over time. The practical importance of this distinction is that, while culture accumulates from the words, thoughts, and actions of leaders over time—and is therefore relatively inaccessible to immediate leadership intervention—climate is immediately accessible. If you sustain and reinforce an intentional change in climate, you drive a change in the culture.

We know from experience and from published social science research which aspects of organizational culture and safety climate are critical to safety excellence. There are several culture dimensions critical to high performance in safety, and they can be grouped into organizational, team, and safety-specific dimensions.

The organizational dimensions

These dimensions are not specific to safety but their strength predicts safety outcomes. They have to do with organizational functioning considered broadly. These dimensions reflect the level of goodwill and trust that underwrite the organization's capacity to function smoothly and efficiently:

- PROCEDURAL JUSTICE—The extent to which the individual worker perceives fairness in interactions with his or her superiors and in the supervisors' decision-making process.
- LEADER-MEMBER EXCHANGE—The relationship that the employee has with his or her supervisor. In particular, this scale measures the level of confidence that employees have that their supervisor will advocate for them, look out for their interest, and things of that kind.
- MANAGEMENT CREDIBILITY—The perception that the things that management says are consistent with the things that management does.
- PERCEIVED ORGANIZATIONAL SUPPORT—The perception of the employee that the organization cares about him, values him, and supports him.

The team dimensions

Team characteristics have both direct and indirect effects on safety outcomes (level of safe behavior, injuries, and injury reporting).

- WORKGROUP RELATIONS—The employee's perception of his or her relationship with others in the workgroup. To what degree do they treat each other with respect, listen to each other's ideas, help one another, and follow through on commitments made?
- TEAMWORK—The extent to which the employee perceives that working with other team members is an effective way to get things done.

The safety-specific dimensions

These elements represent three different links between employees and safety outcomes:

- SAFETY CLIMATE—This scale measures the extent to which the employee perceives the organization has a value for safety performance improvement.
- UPWARD COMMUNICATION—The extent to which communication about safety flows freely upward. In part, the relative presence or absence of the tendency to shoot the messenger (i.e., to punish the bearer of bad news).
- APPROACHING OTHERS—The extent to which employees feel free to speak to one another about safety concerns.

Our research shows that organizations with high scores on these nine dimensions have higher levels of performance generally and better safety performance in particular. Specifically, organizations that score well on these dimensions tend to have lower injury rates and fewer process safety incidents, while organizations that score low on these dimensions tend to have higher injury rates and more process safety incidents.

Interestingly, people in management positions frequently feel more positive about the organization's culture than do people working at lower levels in the organization. Leaders may be unaware of problems in the working interface that the people working there have just come to accept as the way things are done. For example, managers might be satisfied with the way exposures are reported, but frontline employees may feel like important information is not asked for or is hard to deliver. Nevertheless, the employees may just accept this situation as "the way things are done around here." It is necessary, then, to understand the organization's culture from the perspective of the people whose working lives are spent at the working interface. This is where culture has its most immediate impact on safety.

CHANGING THE CULTURE

Managers and supervisors play a critical role in culture change. For good or ill, cultural dimensions reflect organizational relationships.

The characteristics that define "how we do things here" are fundamentally about the relationships that employees have with each other, with their superiors, and with the organization as a whole. Managers and supervisors are the ones who communicate organizational priorities and values and who build relationships with individual team members. Managers and supervisors act as messengers between employees and the organization at large, and their actions signal what is accepted and rewarded. To many employees, managers and supervisors *are* the organization.

Optimally, a culture change initiative would engage the whole organization through a comprehensive strategy of evaluating current functioning, defining the desired culture, and engaging employees at every level through defined behaviors and regular feedback. But managers can also have tremendous influence simply through their day-to-day actions. There are several things you can do as a manager or supervisor to begin changing the culture:

Demonstrate your support

Are you asking employees to take on new roles? To buy in to new safety policies? Engage them in discussions about organization or operational changes and collaborate on solutions to perceived problems. Employees who believe that the organization is concerned about their needs in general, and who perceive that support is available, are also likely to believe in the organization's values and to be actively engaged in its goals.

Strengthen your relationship with reports

Ask how employees are doing, check with them on concerns, and give thoughtful responses to suggestions. Employees who have a good relationship with their supervisors are more likely to be cooperative, to live up to the spirit of organizational objectives (rather than just the letter), and to initiate voluntary contributions.

Show that you're fair

Make sure that policies and procedures that impact your employees, such as promotions or disciplinary actions, are fair, consistent, and visible. Employees who perceive that decisions affecting them are made fairly, even if they don't like the outcome, are more willing to contribute above and beyond their immediate job duties.

Demonstrate credibility

Follow through on commitments to employees, "walk the talk" when it comes to following new procedures, and be open about the reasons behind your decisions. The way in which employees perceive your judgment, honesty, consistency, fairness, and openness in dealing with them influences the extent to which they will take personal responsibility and support new initiatives.

Build stronger workgroups

Set expectations for "fair play" and model them in your own interaction with others. If coworkers treat each other with respect, listen to each other's ideas, help one another out, and follow through on commitments made, they're more likely to become actively engaged in their workgroup's commitments.

Show that the objectives matter

Does your company say safety (or any key performance area) is "number one," but then behave as though production and schedules are what really matter? Evaluate the message of your actions and align them to mirror your stated objectives. The more value that employees see attached to goals, the more likely they will be willing to invest their energy in them.

Encourage communication

Initiate conversations about performance concerns and allow workers to speak without interruption, recognizing the value in their ideas. The more freely communication flows from workers to their supervisors, and among the workers themselves, the more influence an organization has over the level of desired workforce behavior.

LEADING THE CHANGE

Culture change is not easy. Culture changes slowly, yet it is changing all the time. Leaders influence the culture each time they make a decision, leave an issue hanging, take a stand, or address an issue. The change process is about directing and accelerating the natural change that is already happening. Adapting a strategic approach to culture change and safety improvement can help drive the development of an organization where safety really is a driving value and where its managers "lead with safety" to better safety and operational functioning.

CHAPTER TWENTY-SEVEN
ATTRIBUTES OF A CULTURE OF COMMITMENT

*Unless commitment is made, there are
only promises and hopes; but no plans.*
—PETER DRUCKER

As we get better at applying the lessons of the past, we've discovered that safety performance is more complex than a binary equation of "human error" vs. "mechanical failure" and that the configuration of risk extends far beyond the shop floor. Integrating these lessons, however, is an organizational undertaking that will fundamentally challenge the assumptions and practices of a workforce trained to follow rules. This chapter discusses why and how managers need to develop a culture of commitment—a workplace that supports and encourages engagement with the organization's values and creates an environment in which discretionary effort flourishes.

THE DIFFICULTY WITH COMPLIANCE

In safety, organizations, particularly those that work with high-hazard conditions and systems, depend on a high level of compliance with rules and regulations to keep employees safe. Whether the rules govern personal protective equipment (e.g., goggles or special clothing) or pertain to process safety procedures (e.g., control of process changes, maintenance of critical equipment, emergency planning and response), assuring consistent use requires a high level of organizational discipline. But overly depending on this discipline is a little like focusing on blood pressure as the main measure of a person's wellness. It is one indicator, and an important one, but it doesn't tell the whole story. Culture, leadership, organizational systems, and other dimensions make up a complex system that interact with, influence, and ultimately guide safety systems and regulations. There are several barriers that compliance-based safety poses to advancing performance:

Injuries live in the past

Historic injury data, from which we derive the bulk of regulations, are helpful for understanding the types of outcomes that *can* occur when working with particular materials, equipment, or processes. Historic data, however, can never anticipate every possible outcome. And ironically, when our primary source of exposure information is injury, the better we become at preventing injuries, the less information we have to work with. The key to getting in front of this situation is to stop chasing injuries and start focusing on exposure, using the *likelihood* for injury (leading indicator) rather than actual injuries (lagging indicator) as the measure of performance and the trigger for change. Properly measured, exposure gives leaders a chance to intervene before injury occurs and gets them out of the rearview mirror approach to safety.

Culture dominates

Like other business systems, safety activities are interpreted through culture—the unwritten external guide on "how I should behave here." Culture strongly influences how closely people follow explicit rules—or whether they follow them at all. For example, requiring a face shield when grinding may seem straightforward enough. Yet, in some workplaces it could be considered okay or even expected that workers opt out when the boss isn't around. Compliance-based organizations face an additional hurdle when rules based on prior injuries create blind spots. These are the rules that either mandate actions that don't apply to the work or that demand something that is difficult or impossible for the worker to do. Taking the face shield example, "blind spot" rules might require the use of personal protective equipment (PPE) that is routinely stored 100 feet or more away from the grinding area or that may even be unavailable. Behavior, like electricity, follows the path of least resistance. Rules work best when they are aligned with cultural and organizational realities.

Being good at following the rules only means you're good at following the rules

In many organizations the achievement of a low injury rate (or another single measure) is assumed to indicate that safety more generally (specifically including management of process safety and prevention of worker fatalities) is well managed. In fact there is not necessarily any connection between good management of process safety and good management of personal safety. Further, there is not necessarily any connection between injury rates and actual exposure to injury events. Organizations need to be able to understand in real-time what their exposure to risk looks like.

Compliance can't account for all the variables in a live workplace

Rules are static and are usually based on our best understanding of likely exposure to risk in our current configuration of equipment and processes. But live workplaces change, events intersect, things happen. Employees trained to comply with the rules, without a sense of the bigger picture or the principles behind why we do what we do, are not positioned to respond when anomalies do occur. Employees need to understand when exposure is increasing and know how to change their behavior in response. It's counterintuitive but employees do not put themselves at risk unless they receive a positive consequence for doing so. Things like saving time, expending less effort, going home early, and meeting production quotas can often put pressure on rules compliance. We need to understand these pressures and ensure the consequences of compliance are much more positive than the consequences of non-compliance.

So how do organizations advance safety in the face of such complex, and constantly changing, realities? By developing an inherent organizational adaptability to change that extends to every employee in the organization. We call this the culture of commitment.

MAKING WORK MEANINGFUL

A culture of commitment can be defined as an environment in which employees at all levels will do what is right for themselves, their boss, and the organization, even when they would personally gain from non-compliance, because they are bought in and connected to the organization and leaders' vision. When our clients talk about making the transition from compliance to commitment, they are really contrasting "mere compliance" with commitment. They are dissatisfied with the fact that they have employees and contractors who are disengaged, blindly going through the motions, or expending energy to "tick boxes" without generating any value from the exercise. They want to see employees and contractors demonstrate real commitment to the organization's mission, a willingness to challenge processes that limit success, a motivation to perform above and beyond the base requirements of their jobs, and a personal investment that allows them to endure short-term pain for long-term gain.

The solution is not to do away with procedures and process—that would be absurd. The first step is to understand your organization and in particular, how value is created. In safety for example, value comes from reducing exposure to prevent incidents. Value also comes from contributing to organizational culture and leadership, which improves organizational capability. The next step is to ensure that the procedures and processes contribute to adding value, and that the people expected to follow the procedures and processes understand how that linkage occurs. For example, if a procedure calls for replacing a chemical transfer hose monthly, we want to be sure there is a real reason for doing that (e.g., testing has shown that the hose degrades and is vulnerable to rupture.) We should then make sure that people involved in the process understand why it is important (i.e., the consequences of not changing the hose). Finally, we need to empower individuals to exercise judgment, and then equip them with the skill, information, and experience that support excellent decision making (e.g., what happens if a replacement hose is not available when change is due?) This includes:

- Coaching individuals on the places in their work where judgment is desired and empowering them to do so.

- Making sure that team members not only see the connection between their work and the big-picture objectives but also have ways to challenge anything that constrains them from contributing to those objectives.

- Teaching decision makers how to use judgment successfully. They need to understand which decisions are theirs, how to weigh different risks, and how to challenge constraints without risking their reputations or their jobs.

- Making sure that higher-order systems and processes don't punish people for trying to do the right thing well, even when they fail. Forgive negative outcomes of decisions so long as the individuals recognized the situation they were in and made the best judgment they could.

SETTING THE STAGE

It takes time to build a culture of commitment, but leaders can start by posing four simple questions:

1. What is our real goal?

In other words, what is the commitment we are asking people to make? The real goal is not whether you want to be "zero harm" or "injury free" or whether to reduce injuries by 25% in one year or two. These distinctions are important and a part of every safety performance plan. Yet they sidestep the core element of commitment:

The big picture view of what safety means *to us*. How we think about safety, how we see its role in the organization, and what defines success—these things shape everything we do and say. As a start, consider how you define success. Do you judge your safety performance based on the absence of failure? Or do you use a balanced mix of valid leading and lagging indicators when assessing safety performance?

2. Do we understand the state of our culture as it is now? What does our culture encourage?

Culture is an important element of safety success. Organizations that have strong adaptive cultures (basically an openness to change) also tend to have low injury rates. An extensive body of research identifies measurable cultural characteristics that, in addition to predicting safety outcomes (such as level of safe behavior, injury rates, and event reporting), have also been shown to predict variables indirectly related to safety, such as turnover, citizenship behavior, trust in the organization, and trust of employees, innovation, and creativity. How employees perceive these dimensions has been shown to correlate to injury rate.

Under the demands of day-to-day activity, safety technical and management systems will be used rigorously only if people within the organization understand the overall vision for safety and the values that support that vision. In an organization where general functioning is poor, we tend to see them struggling with compliance and organizational commitment is nonexistent. These organizations are also more likely to see compromises and shortcuts in the implementation of safety systems.

3. How good is our safety leadership?

Do we promote a strong adaptive culture or do we inadvertently reinforce (or create) poor organizational functioning? Managers are ultimately responsible for the culture of the organization, whether they've been there for 20 years or have just arrived. Line employees cannot change the culture of the organization; that power is in the hands of the leaders. There are a core set of safety best practices as well as the leaders' transformational style that have a predictive relationship to the culture of an organization and its safety results.

It's easy for us as managers to take the victim approach to the culture. Are we wallowing in the problems or are understanding that we are the change agents for improving organizational functioning? Once we understand the strengths and gaps in our safety leadership behaviors, we can then start focusing on what we are doing well and reinforce these behaviors as well as understand where we can improve. It's easy to believe others judge our intentions based on our words, but what others see and judge is our behaviors.

4. Have we earned the right to engage the hourly workforce?

Commitment is a function of social exchange. Simply, people will treat the organization the way the organization treats them. As leaders, we need to develop relationships with employees as real people not economic units. We need to show that we really care. Earning the right to engage employees is critical to any new endeavor. You see the lack of this step often in poorly-launched, behavior-based safety initiatives where improvement is not a partnership but a steely contest of "us vs. them." In these scenarios you may see data withheld, observations used as the only metric, and little feedback given to observed employees. Not surprisingly, the quality of these efforts is often poor, and if they are sustained at all it is through sheer will. On the other hand, implementations in which leaders work on their own credibility, give employees due recognition and feedback, and generally set their own shoulder to the wheel alongside other employees tend to have workforces who are equally committed to finding exposures and in turn engaging their peers in improving safety.

One of the biggest barriers we have seen to building commitment, particularly in previously compliance-focused organizations, is the improper use of discipline. Usually this is a result of leaders who are frustrated at what they perceive as an employee losing focus or blatantly violating a rule. Discipline has a role in safety (see chapters 13 and 14) but when not applied consistently and fairly it will undermine leadership credibility, the integrity of the rules, and the culture of the organization. If our response to all injuries is to assign blame, employees will quickly disengage from the organization since they perceive it as unjust. This situation also stems from an organization's focus on lagging indicators as their sole measure of safety performance.

BUILDING COMMITMENT

It is important to remember that achieving a culture of commitment doesn't happen overnight. It takes persistent and vigilant attention to safety processes, culture, and leadership. While creating a committed workforce may seem like a monumental undertaking it really comes down to changing just one behavior at a time.

CONCLUSION

As managers and supervisors we are responsible for assuring that the workers who are counting on us for their safety and for whom we are responsible can and do work safely. It is in the common interest of the individual worker, the supervisor and managers in the worker's "chain of command," the worker's union if one is present, the senior executives of the organization, and the organization's board and shareholders that every worker return from work each day as healthy as they were when they began the day.

To fulfill the responsibility as stewards of safety every manager and supervisor must understand what good safety management entails, and that has been the purpose of this book. No book can compile a complete list of solutions covering every leadership challenge that will confront you in your working career. However, we can learn from the experiences of others and take the parts that are useful and apply them.

Every manager need not, and will not, be an expert in the technology of safety engineering and industrial hygiene. But every manager should be aware of how to deploy that expertise to the best advantage and how to assure that the organization's overall management systems contribute to rather than detract from safety objectives.

INDEX

Made in the USA
Columbia, SC
13 June 2017